Chatelaine

EARN SPEND SAVE

The savvy guide to a richer, smarter, debt-free life

by *Chatelaine's* money expert KIRA VERMOND

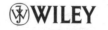WILEY

John Wiley & Sons Canada, Ltd.

Library and Archives Canada Cataloguing in Publication Data

Vermond, Kira
    Earn, spend, save : the savvy guide to a richer, smarter, debt-free life / by Kira Vermond.

Includes index.
ISBN 978-0-470-67654-7

    1. Women—Canada—Finance, Personal. I. Title.

HG179.E37 2009   332.0240082'0971   C2009-905898-7

Production Credits
Cover design: Philina Chan
Interior design: Ian Koo
Typesetting: Pat Loi
Front and back cover photo: Istockphoto.com
Printer: Friesens

John Wiley & Sons Canada, Ltd.
6045 Freemont Blvd.
Mississauga, Ontario
L5R 4J3

Printed in Canada

1 2 3 4 5 FP 13 12 11 10 09

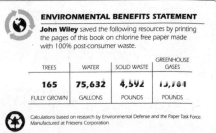

ENVIRONMENTAL BENEFITS STATEMENT

John Wiley saved the following resources by printing the pages of this book on chlorine free paper made with 100% post-consumer waste.

TREES	WATER	SOLID WASTE	GREENHOUSE GASES
165	75,632	4,592	13,781
FULLY GROWN	GALLONS	POUNDS	POUNDS

Calculations based on research by Environmental Defense and the Paper Task Force.
Manufactured at Friesens Corporation

TABLE OF
CONTENTS

....

VII ACKNOWLEDGEMENTS

  I INTRODUCTION: WHY YOU
     NEED TO READ THIS BOOK
  2 Advice you can use
  4 How to read this book

  5 CHAPTER 1: WORK YOUR MONEY
  7 Where you are right now
 II You really are worth it
13 What do you want?
15 Make a good job a money machine
18 No time like flextime
23 Time out after burnout
29 Into the great unknown

30 Find time to network
33 Interview like a pro
36 They Google you
37 How to negotiate a better package
38 Going it alone
41 You're ready

43 CHAPTER 2: SPEND LIKE A PRO
44 Make a budget
54 Skills to pay the bills
59 Every cent counts, count every cent
69 Own or lease a car?
73 Complain and get your money back
76 Next stop: Debt busters

77 CHAPTER 3: DEBT: KNOW WHAT YOU OWE
79 Debt: The trillion-dollar question
80 Good debt vs. bad debt
85 Know your fees
90 Do you debit?
91 Get out of debt—faster!
97 FICO savings
101 The unthinkable: Bankruptcy
104 Watch money grow

105 CHAPTER 4: INVEST IN YOURSELF
107 Should you hire help?
113 Be your own investment advisor
115 Know the terms
121 Start a money club
123 Define your goals
125 How much risk can you take?
126 Big money concepts you can't miss
131 Your best investment deals
137 Keep it going

139 CHAPTER 5: GET YOUR TAX ACT TOGETHER

141 DIY or hire a pro?
144 Tame the paper trail
145 Write it off and save
153 RRSP 1, 2, 3
157 Write-offs for the self-employed
160 What if I file late?
161 When the auditor comes to call
163 Not as taxing as you expected

165 CHAPTER 6: MORTGAGE SWEET MORTGAGE

169 Are you ready to buy?
171 Get your money together
176 Locate an agent
181 Pay down your mortgage fast
184 When it's time to sell
189 Know the terms
196 Another reason to sell

197 CHAPTER 7: MONEY MEETS MARRIAGE

199 Money is something else
204 Why propose a pre-nup?
207 Wedding day lite
209 Combining your finances . . . or not
212 Divorce: In debt do you part
217 Living the common-law life
219 With this money I thee wed

221 CHAPTER 8: EVERYTHING ELSE

223 Making sense of mat leave
230 Kids don't come cheap
231 RESP(ECT) your kids' education

236 Pick your insurance well
243 Save for an emergency
245 Life after a layoff
248 Leaving a legacy: Do some good
251 Where there's a will
257 Your two cents

259 CHAPTER 9: YOUR SIX-MONTH MONEY PLAN

261 Month 1: Lay the foundation
263 Month 2: Track it down
265 Month 3: Make a change
266 Month 4: Save for life
268 Month 5: Plan for emergencies
269 Month 6: Almost done

271 LEARN MORE

271 Calculate it!
272 Earn it!
272 Spend it!
273 Save it!

275 INDEX

ACKNOWLEDGEMENTS

DEVELOPING A PERSONAL FINANCE BOOK FOR Canadian women that covers everything from accrued interest to variable-rate mortgages has certainly been both a labour of love and the ultimate team effort. We would like to offer a huge thank you to all the women who offered us their personal experiences with money, not to mention some tips and tricks that everyone can benefit from: Annemarie Belford, Ann Coyle, Keri-Lyn Durant, Tag Goulet, Laura Haughey, Nancy Hicks, Ruthann Hicks, Marci Hotsenpiller, Lisa Hyman, Christine Kirkland, Erica Pinsky, Ann Rimkus, and Susan Sebekos. Extra thanks go to Amy Baskin, Angie Gallop, Aude Lemoine, Sheryl Spencer, Jane Lewis, Karan Smith, Heather Wright, and, of course, David Carpenter and Dayle Petty for keeping the project on track, and to Jean Mills for putting in so many research hours. Thanks to Kira Vermond for her work writing the book and to Rebecca Caldwell, Leah Fairbank, and Marnie Peters for editing and making the copy sing. Thanks also to Cameron Williamson and Philina Chan for the cover design.

We'd also like to thank the book's reviewers and financial planning aficionados, Judith Cane and Rhonda Sherwood, for their time and effort working with the manuscript. As always, you gave us fantastic advice and context. Keep helping women reach their financial goals! Amanda Mills and Nora Spinks, you're an inspiration to any woman who wants to live life on her own terms and make a buck too.

Keep earning, spending, and saving.

Introduction

WHY YOU NEED TO READ THIS BOOK

···

YOU CAN DO THIS.

Maybe it seems strange to begin a book about personal finance for women with this type of declaration, but let's face it: when it comes to learning the ins and outs of index funds, RESPs, taxes, pre-nups, and mortgages, couldn't we all use a pep talk before digging in?

Here at *Chatelaine* we thought so too. That's why we wrote *Earn, Spend, Save*, a money management book specifically for Canadian women that offers smart, savvy financial advice and tackles the unique financial conundrums that we face.

Here's the thing: as women we live longer than men and need more retirement savings, we are in the paid workforce for fewer years, and we are statistically less likely to ask for a raise or make bucks quite as big as our male counterparts. Not only that, we're our children's primary caregivers, we take on the lion's share of eldercare, and we still run the household even when we're out 9 to 5 (or 6 or 7) bringing home our bacon.

It's partly this time crunch that keeps us from delving in to spending plans or taking stock of stocks, but there's something else at work here. A lot of us say we simply feel unsure or unskilled when it comes to managing our money, despite the fact that numerous studies over the past couple of decades show that women make excellent investors. According to Lisa Hyman, a financial planner in Ottawa, we do more homework before buying, we trade less often, and we are more likely to stay the course.

"Women's investments do better over the long term than men. Women look for a plan and stick to it, whereas men are often looking for the latest hot tip," she says.

So considering we've got what it takes to come out on top, why do so many of us say we would rather sort out our junk drawers than read a prospectus or determine how capital gains actually affect our taxes?

This has to change.

ADVICE YOU CAN USE

Maybe you already invest like a pro, but your credit cards are perpetually warm from too many lunch hour runs to the shopping mall. Or maybe you are control incarnate when it comes to splashy sale signs in shop windows, but think "blue chip" describes a snack that's killer with salsa. Perhaps you want to invest in RRSPs but are still paying down a student loan, looking for ways to save for your kids' education, or are working up the courage to ask your boss for a raise. And what's a bear market again?

You're probably more financially literate than you realize. But let's be honest, nearly everyone can use more education when it comes to getting up to speed on the latest smart money moves. The good news is that you're about to earn a degree in financial self-improvement. Simply by picking up *Earn, Spend, Save*, you are setting the wheels in motion for achieving your financial goals and living the life you want.

Need proof? Try answering these questions:

- What's the difference between a self-directed RESP and a pooled plan?

- Why is it important to check if your bank uses the average daily balance method for calculating minimum balance and interest?

- How much do you actually need in your savings in order to retire comfortably in Canada? (And why is this number different than your partner's?)

- What's the best way to start a financial plan with the love of your life without losing that love in the process?

- When it comes time to apply for a loan, why is 750 the credit score magic number?

- Do men care if you make more money than they do? (The answer might surprise you!)

- What percentage of your gross income should go toward housing costs?

- How can you build a down payment in no time flat with the federal government's Home Buyers' Plan?

- What can you claim under the Children's Fitness Tax Credit?

- Are you a good candidate for a pre-nup? Is *he*?

How many questions could you answer? Read this book from cover to cover, and not only will you be able to flip back to this page and answer every question, but you'll also have the confidence to put your new knowledge into action and make your money work for you.

of infinite managerial wisdom, it's decided that Keri (a.k.a. Workplace Wonder Woman) can take on the tasks of two people, so why bother hiring a replacement for her former position? Soon Keri's workload is cranked to 11. She routinely toils 17-hour days. She even finds herself fantasizing about cigarettes—not because she itches to start smoking, but because it would give her an acceptable excuse to take a break.

But it's not until Keri and her husband Quinn start thinking about having kids that it dawns on her: She's working for a company where "flextime" might as well be the new F-word. And the pay? Add up all the unpaid overtime and she's not making peanuts, she's simply raking in their shells.

So what should Keri do?

    A. *Find a new job that actually meets her financial and personal needs.*

    B. *Work out a six-month financial plan that would enable her to quit her job and hang out her own shingle as a self-employed PR consultant.*

    C. *Walk into her boss's office with a list of proposals and negotiate a bump in pay and a saner work schedule.*

In reality, here's what happened: she chose option B, and now has a house, two kids, and 10 years later, she's making nearly three times the money she did at her old job. The student loan fiasco is a mere memory.

"The day I walked into the office and explained to my boss I would be quitting to go solo he told me, 'You'll be back,' " she says now, grinning. "He just couldn't believe I would give up a solid career to jump into the unknown. Maybe I was being foolishly optimistic, but I'd built up a nest egg, had a plan, and just knew I would succeed. And I did!"

Keri walked away from that long-ago conversation feeling elated, knowing she was finally taking her career, her sanity, and her purse strings, into her own hands.

Y OU DON'T HAVE TO TAKE THE BIG LEAP OUT OF the traditional workforce like Keri to be content at work. (Although you would have our full respect and encouragement if you did.) Maybe you're a kindergarten teacher in Winnipeg and, in a similar situation, would have found a way to negotiate a job share or part-time position. Or perhaps you're a podiatrist in Montreal, a carpenter in Halifax, or a museum curator in Toronto who would rather find new, better employment elsewhere.

Whatever we do during our 20, 40, or 60+ hours on the job each week, as women we all share one indelible truth: we want to take control of our personal finances and live rich, happy, deeply satisfying lives.

Earning a living is the very first step.

Want to know how to do it right? In this chapter we'll walk you through the big picture first. We'll look at what kind of professional life you're living and what you're actually worth to your employer. (Hint: it's more than you can imagine.) Then we'll explore possibilities that are open to you *right now* to make positive changes in your working life, whether it's finding ways to make your current job exciting, fulfilling—and yes, more lucrative—or transitioning to a new job, career, or even a new industry.

Whatever it is you do for a living, or want to do after a hiatus from employment, we're going to remind you to ask yourself a couple of important questions to ensure you're on the right track toward balancing the wealth you earn (in good times and bad) and your life.

What do you say? Let's get the money rolling.

WHERE YOU ARE RIGHT NOW

So you want to change your life. You want to negotiate for more money and benefits, love the job you're in, *and* have time to attend your daughter's soccer practice, dive into that pile of books collecting dust beside your bed, and share more than just a rushed cup of coffee with your husband each morning. Before we figure out how to help you reach these goals, let's step back and take a look at the big picture to examine where Canadian women are at in their quest for sanity at work right now.

According to the Vanier Institute of the Family, based in Ottawa, striking a healthy balance between work and private life has never been so challenging. We're working longer hours, we feel we're unable to "shut off" work even after the day is done, and that little word "overloaded?" Well, it doesn't even begin to describe how we typically feel.

In fact, between 46 and 61 percent of working parents say they have a hard time juggling work and family commitments because, between the computer, the BlackBerry, and the slippery slope of shifting work hours, job commitments encroach on the rest of the day. In his report *Family Life and Work Life: An Uneasy Balance*, Roger Sauvé, a Vanier Institute of the Family contributor, found that personal time has definitely suffered at the expense of work—and forget being compensated for the extra burden. For instance:

- The average amount of time working Canadians spend with family members on a workday has fallen 45 minutes since 1986. Add it up and that's about *190 hours* each year.

- The amount of time Canadians spend at work increased by 54 hours a year between 1992 and 2005.

- The average hourly earnings of workers in 2008 had not increased since 1984, although families are bringing in more money in total since additional family members are working at more jobs.

Women experience an even bigger time crunch each day. Although Statistics Canada data shows that more men are willing to throw in a load of laundry, take out the trash, care for the kids, and wipe down the fridge, women still end up taking on the lion's share of housework and child care—even though they're spending more hours at work than in the past.

And there are a lot more of us now playing out this particular drama. Canadian women have one of the highest labour force participation rates in the world, a rate that has caught up with that of men. Yes, we've come a long way, baby, but it also seems that our collective GPS has steered us down a very bumpy road.

Okay, now that we have the numbers to prove what we've been feeling in our gut all along—that we're painfully stretched over a chasm between work and life commitments—what does it mean to our bottom line?

Quite a lot, as it turns out. Let's go back to Keri's story for a moment. Anybody can see that she was seriously overworked and underpaid. Yet it took her years to break out of her professional rut and find the courage to stand up for herself and release herself from a bad job.

Why did it take her such an inordinately long time to find a solution? We have a couple of theories. For starters, Keri honestly saw her job as a stepping stone to something bigger and better, but as time went on and she outgrew the position, she never stopped to re-evaluate whether her thoughts about the job still reflected reality.

And there is another, even more obvious reason for staying stuck: Keri was simply too stressed, too tired, and too burnt-out by the end of the day to take a step back and look at her own life. She knew there was something wrong, but didn't have the energy to figure out what.

Not that we want to blame Keri. Absolutely not. As the numbers show, most of us have been in her shoes at one time or another and know what a treadmill feels like as it's chugging along under our feet. But (and this is a big but) if we find the time to step off, even for only two nights with a case of Red Bull at our side, and take stock of our working life, it's amazing what new paths we can envision for ourselves—paths that pay.

So let's say Keri had taken a week off work years ago and used the time to do a little internal digging to see if she was indeed being underpaid. Surprise! She was. If she had walked into her boss's office and negotiated even a small raise, that conversation could have been a valuable first step in helping Keri save big on needless expenses. Here's why:

Let's say Keri's student loan is worth $30,000. She decides to take seven years to pay it off. Every month the bank automatically deducts $452.87 from her account to hack down the loan. But then Keri scores a small raise equalling just $58.70 each month. She's tempted to have fun with the tiny windfall, but instead uses it to help delete her debt. The result? Keri's student loan is paid off one full year faster, and the total borrowing cost is *$1,208.04 less.*

Dream on, though, if you think your boss will ever tap your shoulder after an important meeting and say, "The way you convinced that client to sign on for another five years? That was stellar. What'd ya say we give you a raise?" No. It is up to us to negotiate a salary that reflects our fabulous work ethic, our superhuman ability to multitask, and our personal commitment to the job—rushing to a patient's side as a nurse or demonstrating unlimited patience as an elementary school teacher. So why do so many of us wait for the shoulder tap?

Erica Pinsky, a workplace harassment and conflict consultant in Vancouver, struggles with this question all the time, particularly when she tries to gauge how much she should charge for speaking engagements or even her hourly consulting rate. She says for years she didn't raise her rates at all and when she finally did, they went up a measly $5 an hour.

"I have colleagues saying I should charge quite a bit more now that I have a book coming out," she says. "And I just don't know. Even when I know what male colleagues are charging, I wonder, 'Could I really charge that much?' "

Others who have studied the phenomenon of women underearners—those who make less money than they want, despite possessing the smarts to earn more—think demanding less at work is partially tied up with our feelings of self-worth. According to Barbara Stanny, the author of *Overcoming Underearning: A Five-Step Plan to a Richer Life*, underearners often can't pay the bills, have few assets, do a lot of unpaid work, and rarely save for the future. (Sound familiar, Keri?) In a nutshell, being an underearner is fundamentally an issue of failing to value ourselves.

"We give away our skills, knowledge, experience and wisdom for free or at bargain prices because there's a little voice in our heads that says, 'Who do you think you are? You don't deserve more than that,'" she says.

Whether you fit the classic description of an underearner, or simply chicken out every time you think about negotiating a raise, the problem with listening to that little voice in our heads is that it's wrong. Dead wrong.

YOU REALLY ARE WORTH IT

Rachel takes a sip of water and realizes she needs to stretch her legs. She's a high-level executive for a cosmetics company, and the weekly marketing meeting is dragging on longer than usual. The problem: The team, primarily made up of men in their forties and fifties, is trying to decide which new ad campaign to go with. It's not that they're stymied by choice. Far from it. Instead, the group is getting caught up in minutiae concerning one of the options.

Rachel quietly drums her fingers on the desk and speaks up.

"These are all interesting points, but we should move on to the next alternative. I'll be honest. I don't think this ad campaign is going to fly. Your average 46-year-old woman is not going to identify with this person," she says, pointing to the photo showing a young slip of a model holding face cream. "Our customer wants to see herself in that picture, only better."

The team moves on.

As someone who has long held powerful positions at companies, Rachel knows she adds an extra element of wisdom to many such conversations. And the organizations she has worked for know it too, particularly those that go out of their way to ensure more women climb their ranks into positions of influence.

Why? It's all about diversity, not simply in terms of tipping a hat to gender, race, colour, or creed, but as something that truly contributes to the company's bottom line: diversity of thought. Employers who embrace the idea that people with diverse backgrounds, particularly at the managerial level, can best solve problems are discovering that it pays.

"Don't get me wrong, I can talk their talk," says Rachel of the men she works with, "but I speak another language too."

Although it's no secret that women are still under-represented in the business world, you may be surprised that industry is starting to wake up to the fact that a multitude of studies, surveys, and reports all seem to point to one awe-inspiring conclusion: women are good for business. We're talking good in the dollars and cents meaning of the word, not because we serve a mean cup of coffee or look good in a skirt.

In its 2009 *Groundbreakers* report, Ernst & Young brought together findings from numerous sources to make that exact point. For instance, data from a 2007 Catalyst report found that, on average, Fortune 500 companies with more women on their boards of directors saw better financial performances than those with fewer women on their boards. It also cited a 2007 McKinsey study showing that companies with three or more women in senior management scored higher than companies with no women at the top tier when measuring workplace excellence.

"Investing in women to drive economic growth is not simply about morality or fairness. It's about honing a competitive edge," said Lou Pagnutti, Ernst & Young's chairman and CEO, when releasing the report during the darkest days of the 2009 recession. "There is opportunity during this time of adversity—it's time we recognize that and build women into the leadership fabric of our organizations. Diversity is not a 'nice to have.' It's a business imperative."

Even as far back as 2000, when University of Michigan Business School professor Theresa Welbourne analyzed 1,400 rapidly growing IPO companies, she found that the initial stock price, stock price growth, and growth in earnings over a three-year period were higher when there were more women in executive positions. She agreed that a diverse management team made a difference, but also concluded that when women are in top jobs, they also have a positive impact on communication within the company.

Now consider the coming labour shortage that will occur as baby boomers retire in droves without enough younger employees to replace them. Can you blame employers for looking to *you* as a way to fill positions with skilled workers and boost profits simultaneously?

WHAT DO YOU WANT?

So studies prove that you not only have a lot on your plate, but also that, because you have a different take on the world, you add real monetary value to a company's bottom line. Knowing all this can make it much easier to negotiate better pay, sane work hours, or anything else you need to be successful.

But what exactly does that success look like, and what kind of steps do you need to take to get you there?

It's time to set this book down for 30 minutes, grab a pen and some paper, and settle in with a cup of green tea to keep your brain cells firing on every last cylinder. (In other words, save the champagne for the day you reach your goals.) Figuring out the next step to the rest of your life is going to take some thinking, so prepare yourself to be focused, comfortable, and eager to dig deep.

Ready? Now, take two pieces of paper and write the following two sentences, one on each page:

What is my life like right now?

If I had a magic wand, what would my perfect life look like?

Write anything that comes to you. Anything at all. Just remember to include your work life, personal life, and financial situation. Is your current state of affairs like Keri's before she gave her professional life a total overhaul? Are you feeling stressed to the max, torn in two or three places and with little financial savings to show for it? Or perhaps you left your job years ago to care for your kids and now you're thinking you want back into the world of grown-up conversation around a boardroom table. (And the money would be nice too.)

Now flip to the next page. Where would you like to see yourself in your professional, personal, and financial spheres? Do you want to be working for a progressive company where some employees share jobs (by choice), make their own hours, and take Friday afternoons off in the summer? Maybe you're looking for a promotion, or know it's time to leave your current workplace to set up your own business.

Look at what's written on your two pages. How different is your current reality from your dream life? Do you just need to make a nip or a tuck to your existing job? Then read on to grab some exciting pointers aimed at helping you negotiate your way into better pay and benefits. You'll also get the financial lowdown on life-balancing perks including flexible hours and even sabbaticals.

If you're thinking about making even more drastic changes, there's insight for you too. We'll give you tools, direct from the pros, that will help you find and land the job you never even knew you wanted. (And, later in the book, we'll teach you what to do if the job you have suddenly disappears.)

As we've discussed, these goals are not only possible, they *must* happen for everyone's sake. Yes, statistics show that as a smart, savvy woman, you're in demand. Employers need you. You deserve to aim high and fulfill your ambitions without anyone throwing obstacles in your path. But the data also proves one more point: that something's got to give.

MAKE A GOOD JOB
A MONEY MACHINE

All it takes is one phone call from her mother to turn Jane's career around. Jane, an assistant manager for a large farmers' market in Ontario, spends 20 minutes on the telephone itemizing all the reasons she wants to quit her job—the petty politics, the long hours, and her low salary—when her mother finally interrupts her mid-sentence.

"But you like the work itself, right?" she asks.

That's when it hits Jane. She doesn't just like the work, she loves it, she's good at it, and when push comes to shove, she can't imagine working anywhere else.

"That's when I knew I had to make the job I already had the job I've always wanted," Jane says.

Determined to build a bridge, not a gangplank, Jane approaches her boss, calls a meeting with her colleagues, and speaks openly and honestly about how workplace politics is making it hard to get the job done. Although one employee leaves the meeting in a huff, the remaining actually agree. As a group, the employees decide to start afresh and work together. They even begin to plan a harvest season picnic for their families come August.

With the political wrangling taken care of, Jane knows she still has one more conversation to go: she needs to negotiate better hours and pay with her manager. And after a little research, she's ready.

Until Jane determined what was holding her back at work—and tackled the problem—she embodied what career consultants see as an epidemic amongst professional women: the tendency to work hard and wait for the reward that might never come. She's not the only one. Studies consistently show that the compensation discrepancy between men and women can be boiled down to three little words: women don't ask.

But we must. It's imperative we negotiate for what we need, or risk facing extreme consequences. One U.S. study has shown that by simply accepting what she's offered rather than negotiating for more, the average woman sacrifices more than half a million dollars over the course of her career. That's an incredibly pricey penalty to pay in exchange for avoiding 15 minutes of uneasiness.

So, let's talk about talking about money. While asking for a raise at work requires prep, skill, a fallback plan, and a dose of good timing, it also requires that you remember two basic facts that many of us forget when broaching the subject. A pay increase is dependent on whether you're good at your job and whether you're in demand. Everything else is secondary.

Knowing these two criteria, Jane:

1. Builds her case by listing all of her accomplishments since starting her job two years ago. She's not boastful. She lets the numbers talk.

2. Confirms that few people in her area have her skill set, which combines organic gardening, business, and marketing. She's a perfect fit for her job.

Timing is key, of course. And because Jane doesn't get an annual salary review she's going to have to choose a time when her manager isn't thinking about 20 other tasks or heading out for the weekend. So she scratches Monday morning and Friday afternoon off the calendar. But Thursday morning? Perfect. She shoots out an email asking to meet then.

The chat goes well because Jane is able to prove she's a good employee with competitive qualifications. Not only that, but the organic movement is hot, so the market is raking in new vendors willing to pay extra to set up stalls. Jane's timing couldn't have been better. The upshot? A sweet 15 percent raise.

WORK IT OUT!

Money isn't the only thing you might want to negotiate. Drag out your behemoth benefits document (you know, the tome that you quickly scanned when you took the job and that is now collecting dust in your bottom drawer?) and find out what you're actually receiving. At the very least you'll find a perk you forgot you had and want to use now (Yes! Three hundred dollars worth of massage therapy per year), or, just as likely, there's something you'll want to change. Look out for:

- Dental insurance
- Vision insurance
- Life insurance and accidental death insurance
- Vacation time
- Sick and personal days
- Flextime, job sharing, and telecommuting options
- RRSPs
- Profit sharing
- Pension plans
- Employee Assistance Programs
- Tuition reimbursement
- Health club reimbursement
- Parking and commuting costs
- Adoption benefits
- BlackBerry or wireless reimbursement ■

NO TIME
LIKE FLEXTIME

Money is nice, and so are better benefits. But what happens if your company is in no position to pony up, or if you realize that a few more salary dollars will tip you into a new tax bracket and all that extra income will be hauled away by the taxman? Maybe it's time to think about the value of alternative options such as flexible hours, telecommuting, job sharing, or a compressed workweek, particularly if these perks would make your life easier.

Flextime is by far the most popular perk at work.

Put simply, flextime is, well, flexible time. It can mean starting the day at 7 a.m. and heading out early to pick up the kids at school each afternoon. Or maybe it's a compressed workweek where you're on the job longer hours Monday through Thursday and take every other Friday off. Or perhaps it simply means heading out to the doctor in the afternoon and making up the time later. Particularly for women with a seemingly endless list of outside obligations, flextime is a godsend.

Liking this option? You're not alone. Job flexibility picked up steam in the late '90s as organizations ranging from Hewlett-Packard to IBM, PricewaterhouseCoopers, and Best Buy Co., Inc. declared themselves flexibility focused—possibly in response to studies indicating that a growing number of workers would happily pass up more money for more free time. Today upwards of 70 percent of all employers offer some sort of job flextime option.

Christine Kirkland, human resources operations manager at IKEA Canada in Burlington, says she feels much more positive about her employer—in fact, about her whole life—simply because she knows she's got the flexibility to take care of personal issues during traditional office hours without raising the eyebrows of the higher-ups.

"The flexibility means a lot to me. It takes a lot of the stress off," says Ms. Kirkland, who has tried out the whole gamut of flexible options. "For family life, it's great. There's harmony at home and I'm just generally happier."

WHAT DOES A FLEXIBLE WORK PLAN LOOK LIKE?

Once you've done your homework, a formal written plan should include answers to these questions:

- What is your role in the company?
- What are your accomplishments?
- Who are your customers and what do you do for them?
- What will your new schedule look like? (Be specific.)
- How will customers and colleagues be affected by your schedule?
- How will daily issues be solved if you're not physically at the workplace when they arise? Who will handle them when you're away?
- Who else has this arrangement? (You don't have to name names if privacy is a concern. The number of people in a department or company should be enough.)
- How will this affect the company's bottom line? (Flextime is free, by the way.)
- How flexible will you be? Can you come to emergency meetings?
- How will your compensation change?
- Are there times in the year that your schedule can change to accommodate your employer?
- Are you willing to treat the new work schedule as a pilot project?

This article first appeared in *Today's Parent*, December 2005. ■

"I knew he'd never pay me that kind of money even though I deserved it," says Heather. "But to be honest, even if he'd turned around and said, 'Okay, let's do it,' I didn't want to stay. That definitely made it easy to ask for what I wanted!"

WORK IT OUT!

Moonlighting. If you've ever thought about getting a little money on the side, you're not the only one. A recent survey from south of the border reveals a startling fact: if working women had more available time, many of them would rather get a second job than exercise, take a class, or even get more sleep! Moonlighting is a fabulous way to build a new career, develop skills, meet new people, store some much-needed cash in your cookie jar, and chase dreams without doing a fiscal U-turn.

Yes, some of these ideas require stepping out of your comfort zone (and in one case, your clothes), but nobody said making money is a walk in the park. Unless you become a part-time dog walker.

Here are a few ideas to get you thinking:

- Sell your stuff on eBay or Craigslist
- Have a garage sale
- Sell your crafts for profit
- Pose as a life model for an art class
- Become a TV or film extra
- Place advertising banners on your blog
- Become a mystery shopper
- Sign up to become an online tutor ■

TIME OUT
AFTER BURNOUT

It's 8:30 a.m. and Priya, an executive director for an environmental charitable organization in Manitoba, is already exhausted. She pulls out her BlackBerry and checks the calendar to see what's in the hopper for the day. There's one meeting at 9 a.m., another at 11, a lunch meeting at 12:30, and two lengthy conference calls in the afternoon she still has to prepare for. And somewhere between all the lip flapping and responding to urgent emails and phone messages, she's got to find time to actually get her work done. It looks like it's going to be another gruelling day bound to stretch deep into the evening hours.

She just hopes her seven-year-old daughter won't be too disappointed that they'll have to put off shopping for new school shoes . . . again.

Priya is cranky. She's irritable. Her neck muscles are so tight she's been having a hard time turning her head. And sleep? Forget about it. Priya is also starting to notice her colleagues are walking on eggshells around her, tentatively knocking on her office door and quickly leaving again as soon as the conversation is over. Until now, Priya has always seen herself as a leader and an inspiration to others, not someone people avoid in fear that she'll take their head off over some small infraction.

Anyone can see that Priya is suffering from job burnout and that she needs to make changes in her life so she can go back to being both happy and productive. But if the old saying is true—that a change is as good as a rest—can we also infer that change can actually come in the form of that rest?

Enter the sabbatical.

Sabbaticals—paid or unpaid leave, generally stretching from a month to a year, with a job still waiting on the other side—were once regarded as a perk for the academic set or for business executives with enough clout to demand a few months off to write a book or sail around the world. (Think the ultimate alternative work arrangement, on steroids.) But no longer. A growing number of Canadians, including women just like you, are opting to step away from their computers, grouting tools, or nurses' stations, and demand job arrangements that will help find a way to balance work and life.

A few years ago a Canadian survey by Hewitt Associates, an international human resources consulting firm with offices in Canada, found that 12 percent of employers offered paid sabbaticals and 44 percent offered unpaid leave. And those figures were expected to rise over the coming years.

This growing number of employers offering long leaves is in response to the coming tight labour market and shrinking talent pool, they say. In other words, organizations that already see the writing on the wall are trying to find ways to attract and retain their top talent because they understand one hard-hitting fact: it's much easier and cheaper in the long run to allow employees to take a break than it is to replace burnt-out workers with fresh blood.

So that's what is in it for them. What about you?

Sandra, a senior-level manager for a utilities company in Calgary, jumped on a six-month sabbatical offer after her organization merged and she took a lead role in smoothing over the political fallout.

"It was like herding cats," she says now. "Very, very angry cats. They needed a lot of handholding."

For four months Sandra worked 16-hour days and got by on five hours of sleep nightly. By the time she saw the light at the end of the tunnel, she was ready to call it quits for good. But, surprisingly, when Sandra approached her boss to hand in her resignation, he wouldn't take it. Instead he offered Sandra a half year off, unpaid, to rest, rejuvenate, and rekindle her professional and personal passions.

"I slept for the first two weeks, then joined a book club, signed up for an art class and actually used my local gym membership. It was fantastic," she says, mentioning she even went after a dream that she'd been harbouring for years: to become a children's book author. "I discovered I make a much better manager than a writer," she quips. "But how would I have known that if I hadn't had the time to find out?"

How indeed? If you spend the time wisely, an extended break could revitalize your present career or help launch a new one, assist you in exploring what you're truly gifted at, or allow you to go back to school and uncover new passions or unearth forgotten ones. A sabbatical gives you the time to think about what you want to do next with your life. (Remember those work-life-money questions you answered at the beginning of this chapter? They're a great place to start that internal digging while on sabbatical.) At the same time, sabbaticals help you feel sane again, rather than like a sack of marbles worried about an impending heart attack. You could even travel and reconnect with your spouse, siblings, sons, daughters, or friends.

Remember them?

Yes, to a time-starved 35-year-old gal who lives and dies by her to-do list, the thought of all this free time seems downright, well, pornographic (or at least akin to indulging in a reoccurring lottery-win fantasy). But this dream is actually attainable.

For Sandra, it meant that she realized she wanted to come back to the company and continue to nurture her talents there. If you take a sabbatical, though, you might find, like some others do, that you are much more drawn to a new career as, say, a personal coach for mid-life mothers, a pathologist for hearing-impaired kids, or even as an attorney hell-bent on negotiating a contract in your client's favour.

So yes, you can do it. (If you're wondering how to convince your employer to let you take the leap without scaring her into thinking you won't be back, flip back to page 16 to get the

It's five months after Priya came back to work from her sabbatical and she is feeling happier, lighter, and in control of her days. While away from work she developed perspective with the help of an executive life coach, and discovered she could say no to redundant meetings. She learned to stand up for herself.

"Even though my organization doesn't have a sabbatical program per se, when I approached my board of directors about taking a period of leave, they took one look at my face and said, 'We're so happy this is what you're asking for. We were all worried you were going to quit!' " Priya says now. "But I'll tell you, as soon as we agreed on the date I would take leave, I automatically began feeing better. I had something to look forward to."

Priya also discovered something else amazing: going on sabbatical can actually be a savvy financial move.

Because Priya's job consisted of countless day-to-day administrative tasks that could be divided amongst other employees in her absence, her position became largely redundant. At first this looked like a negative for Priya. But as it turned out, the opposite was true.

Now that she's back at her desk, she is carving out a new position for herself with all her new-found time. It's a more strategic, long-term-thinking kind of role and, because it's the sort of work she loves, she's better at it. In response to her good work—she has found ways to land some large corporate donations—she even got a raise. Priya has never been happier.

"Who knew hitting a wall at work would lead me to this place?"

Sometimes we need the catalyst of a temporary change to make another one permanent. And sometimes that change, rest, or whatever you want to call it, can lead to more money, a more fulfilling job, and—what we all seem to be after—more time.

WORK IT OUT!

Wondering how to plan for a sabbatical that will involve sitting on a sunny beach and re-evaluating your life (or at least a week in New York sans kids)? Here's what you shouldn't do: *over* plan. At least not at the beginning of the process.

That's right. If you try to map out every single detail of your route to freedom, chances are you'll psyche yourself out and wind up deciding against taking that sabbatical. (Your mortgage seems too big to take any financial risk. Your co-workers would be lost without you. How will you explain the leave to your mother? You fill in the blanks.) Replace thinking about *how* you'll pull it off with *why* you need the break—and leave ruminating about those nitpicky details until after you've committed yourself 100 percent to the cause. ■

INTO THE GREAT UNKNOWN

Let's face it, there are times when a pay raise, better hours, or even a sabbatical just isn't enough to keep you happy in your job. Between a boss who talks incessantly about his new car, a soul-sucking commute, and the growing feeling that you work for the "Department of Redundancy Department," sometimes you just need to get *out*.

From finding time for networking, to interviewing like a pro, to controlling what potential employers read about you online, here's how to turn those flight fantasies into a career with staying power.

FIND TIME
TO NETWORK

*It's only a few minutes after 5:30 on a breezy Monday evening
and women holding swishy laptop bags are flooding through
the doors of a hotel conference room in Halifax. Checking a
coat, grabbing a name badge, and lifting a glass of wine, the
attendees are ready to work the room.*

*By the time the canapés are gone and the veggie tray is picked
clean, the nearly 200 businesswomen take their seats for the
formal presentation at this "pink-collar" networking event. And
for the next 45 minutes everyone who stands at the podium
utters what soon becomes the mantra of the evening:*

*"Thank you so much for coming. We know how little time
you have."*

A sea of coifed heads nod.

For most women, finding the time to network can be daunting. Between longer hours behind the desk, increased time on
the road, and juggling daycare, homework, and the odd hot
meal on the table, it can feel downright impossible to squeeze
it in. But women know that networking is important to finding
a better job and advancing in their careers. Really important.

In fact, some data suggests that up to 80 percent of all
job vacancies are never advertised. So how do the positions
get filled? People just like you network their way into them.
Still, although as women we instinctively know exchanging
cards and asking the all-important question—What can I do
for you?—can mean the difference between languishing in a
dead-end career and sailing into workplace nirvana, how do
we find the time?

Here's how: change the way you network and make networking work for the life *you* lead.

Ultimately, one of the best ways to find time to network is
by rethinking the very concept of what a networking event is.

Nora Spinks, the president of Work-Life Harmony Enterprises in Toronto, says some of her clients are creative in how they network. One organizes monthly potluck dinners with other women that rotate from house to house so mothers don't have to be away from their kids in the evening. Others connect by conference call, run book clubs at home, network at the PTA, and even work out together. These are options anyone can try, whether they work in a big city or a small town.

Formal or informal, successful networking happens only when we set boundaries. So don't go to a cocktail reception, seminar, or local meet-and-greet without a clear sense of what you want to get out of the meeting and when you want to leave. If your goal is to be at home when your kids go to bed, make sure you leave in time to say good night. Chances are, you won't be the only one checking her watch at 7:30 and making a mad dash for the door.

"We're getting more creative and innovative in the way in which we're networking," says Spinks. "And we're getting more respectful of each other's time. That's really important."

And what about social networking? Does it work too? Whether you're plugged in to Facebook, LinkedIn, or any other of the myriad of social networking sites, they're definitely a busy woman's best friend.

The upside of these websites is that they're a quick and painless way to spread the word to many people that you're on the market. (And you don't have to spend a small fortune on a new shirt or shoes to impress fellow event attendees.) Daisy Wright, a certified career management coach in Brampton, Ont., is a big believer in social media because she says she has seen it help clients find jobs.

"I'm on LinkedIn and Twitter, and amazing opportunities come to me through social media too. I don't see that diminishing any time soon," she says. For instance, many hiring managers and recruiters send out calls via social media stating what position they're hiring for and what they're looking for in candidates. Other times friends and family might send out information about a vacant position at work that normally wouldn't be widely advertised.

The downside is that, unless you keep a rather closed network of friends, colleagues, clients, and acquaintances, the network can actually become too unwieldy. Referrals are meaningless if the relationship is too distant and you have no way to really know if the person you're referring would be a star employee or a pain in the neck. Rather than tweeting everyone with a, "Here's a job you might be interested in and feel free to tell them I sent you," send job leads only to people you've either worked with or those you've heard stellar things about.

WORK IT OUT!

It's easy to say yes to too many networking opportunities. Before agreeing to any event—even a virtual one sent by a Facebook friend—take a moment to ask yourself some questions and conduct a small investigation before you RSVP.

- Can you get access to the list of people who will be attending? If so, plan in advance whom you would like to meet.

- Are there people on the guest list that could eventually help you land a dream job? Are the attendees decision makers in your desired industry? (You can attend a lot of networking events with few results if your experience level and skill set are out of synch with the other guests.)

- How much time will there be to meet and greet? If there isn't at least an hour of face-to-face time, scrap it. ■

INTERVIEW LIKE A PRO

Of course working the room isn't the only time you'll be required to open your mouth and speak your piece. At some point you're going to land an interview for the job you've been coveting for ages and, after the first flush of jubilation fades, panic could set in.

We would love to tell you to relax, and that all will be well, but we'd better not. In fact, you should feel a few butterflies walking through the interviewer's door, because this chat you're about to have is . . . a . . . very . . . big . . . deal. Goodbye to the days when HR managers read resumés and generally knew who they planned to hire before anyone ever got a chance to speak. No. Today's employers, at least the ones people want to work for, are dead serious when it comes to questioning candidates and extracting answers. And they should be, says Ross Macpherson, an interview coach and resumé expert in Whitby, Ont., who frequently coaches women on the finer points of gab.

"Now, when companies realize it can cost them $40,000 in recruiting fees and job training to hire someone new, they want to make the right decision the first time," he says.

So, as it turns out, you're not the only one feeling the heat the moment you're called in to the room. Do you want to turn that knowledge around and use it to your advantage? We know you know the basics of prepping for that interview—from researching the company's website to showing up on time, or, even better, 15 minutes early—but here are a few other interviewing tips that you probably haven't thought of, but that interview coaches swear by:

PUT IN THE TIME

Prepare, prepare, prepare. We know. You say you've heard this advice a thousand times, but have you ever thought about *exactly* how much time and attention you need give to the interview process?

"People generally spend more time on their outfit than what they're going to say in an interview. It's scary," Macpherson admits.

It's true. People will typically dedicate 30 or 40 hours to tweaking a resumé, but will spend only a half hour preparing for an interview. This despite knowing that interviews are where final decisions are made and where the hiring managers pick the winner! If this is a job you truly desire, spend at least a full day anticipating everything from the tough questions ("Give us three reasons why we should hire you and two why we shouldn't.") to the downright weird ("If there was a billboard with your face on it and three words to describe you, what would they be?"). You can't anticipate every scenario, but you can try to hit the ones most likely to come up.

ACT LIKE AN EMPLOYEE

Say your potential employer is planning to open a new branch in Dubai and wants to hire someone to spearhead the project. If you show up with recent magazine or newspaper articles in hand about challenges other companies have already faced there—and offer possible solutions—you're already proving your worth. It's harder for an employer to dismiss a person who is already acting like a team player.

TAKE A NUMBER

"Hello. Welcome to interview session three. Please take a seat beside the other candidates in the room. We will be interviewing you together."

Huh?

Honestly, between behavioural interviews, trendy multiple mini-interviews, and, yes, group interviews in which many candidates are corralled into a room to answer questions en masse, there's a chance you'll be asked wacky questions and put into odd situations when you show up for your interview. All you can do is bolster your self-confidence by reminding yourself that women like you are in demand. Take your time before you speak, think about what you're going to say, and smile. (Just don't let them see you cross your fingers behind your back.)

RECOGNIZE YOUR SENSITIVITIES

If you've been fired twice in the past 10 years, you probably don't want anyone to ask you if you've ever been let go. Rather than stumble over your answer, however, keep your head up and answer honestly. Practice what you're going to say before the interview and you'll sound more confident. If pressed for more info, quickly explain what you've learned from the experience. Then move on already.

Still worried the new company might hold the termination against you? Just remember this: Jobs are a lot like marriages. Loads of people get divorced, but that doesn't stop other people from dating them again.

KNOW THYSELF

We'll admit it too: the job interview is a downright abnormal experience. Other than a blind date, in what other circumstance are you expected to walk into a room, meet a complete stranger, and talk about yourself in glowing terms for an hour and a half? But just because it isn't typical, doesn't mean you have to struggle through it.

Here's a tip to get you started: write the ideas you want to get across in the interview in point form then practice telling the story in a few different ways. (You should probably have between six and eight "stories" in mind heading into the interview.) You'll be prepared without sounding like you're giving canned answers.

If you still have a hard time talking about yourself, use your prep time to practice and practice some more. Grab a friend, a spouse, or someone else you're comfortable with to lend an ear. Interview coaches, who range in price from $75 to $150 an hour and up, are a good bet if you're willing to pay.

THEY GOOGLE YOU

Kim, a television producer in Toronto, thought she had the best candidate for the job. He was polite, had experience, and just seemed to fit with the rest of the staff. But that opinion did a 180 degree turn the moment she decided to Google him.

"A news article came up about this candidate reporting he had been charged a couple of years ago for savagely beating someone up during a sporting event," she says now. "We decided to take a pass."

Googling potential employees isn't the only high-tech way that employers are now informally screening candidates. With one in five companies saying they also use social networking sites in the hiring process, according to CareerBuilder.com, it pays to know what kind of incriminating evidence they're trying to find out about you. Their top areas of concern include:

- Information about alcohol or drug use
- Inappropriate photos or information posted on a candidate's page
- Poor communication skills
- Bad-mouthing of former employers or fellow employees
- Inaccurate qualifications
- Unprofessional screen names
- Notes showing links to criminal behaviour
- Confidential information about past employers

On the upside, the study did show that 24 percent of hiring managers found information that helped them make the decision to give a candidate a job. So, particularly if you're looking for work and have accepted potential work or boss friend requests, treat your Facebook page like the ultimate cover letter and show the world how well rounded, interesting, and professional you are.

WORK IT OUT!

Build one of the best self-marketing tools that will help you stand apart from the crowd: a web resumé or web portfolio. With the majority of employers now researching potential hires online, creating a professional, well-designed website about your work is bound to give you the competitive edge. In fact, its very existence speaks to the fact that you are proactive and innovative—not a bad way to sell yourself. The cost to build one ranges from free (if you don't mind an out-of-the-box version and the knowledge that your site will look like a lot of other people's—you might have to pay a small monthly fee eventually), to thousands of dollars for a professionally designed site specific to you. ∎

HOW TO NEGOTIATE A BETTER PACKAGE

You've networked your pumps off, wowed HR, passed the Google search test, and you've got the job. Congratulations. Now comes the fun part: negotiating pay and benefits. Yes, we're still talking about negotiating your way to that half million dollars. While many of the tips back on page 16 apply here too, when it's time to talk money and perks for a new position, there are a few further points to consider:

- **In your court.** Keep in mind that by the time you've received the call saying you've got the job, you are actually in a very good position to ask for a better benefits package. From the employer's standpoint, the recruitment process has been time-consuming and expensive. If they are offering you the position, they sincerely hope you will take it.

- **Ask now, not later.** It's important to make your demands before you start the job. As the job candidate of choice, you are being seen in the best possible light—in other words, you're the "winner"—so the employer is more likely to give you what you want.

- **The money question.** Not convinced the salary is high enough? Unless you are being seriously lowballed, sometimes it's in your best interest to take on a job that pays slightly less than what you're after. However, this tactic makes sense only if you take a job at a company that offers room for advancement. Just two or three promotions and pay increases over the next few years and you'll be making much more money than that initial salary. Of course if the starting salary isn't enough to pay the bills or allow you to save anything for an emergency fund or retirement, by all means walk away.

GOING IT ALONE

Sabrina runs her own business as a personal chef in Calgary. But she hasn't always been self-employed. At one time she worked at a high-end restaurant, but when it suddenly shut down and put her out of work, she had to scramble. She didn't relish finding a new job in the high-octane, hectic-paced industry where nights are always booked and sleep is an afterthought.

"So I licked my wounds for a couple of days then I started thinking about what else I could do," she says. "I realized I could combine my cooking skills with my passion for making people's lives more enjoyable."

*Sabrina targets busy working women who are willing to shell
out for a good leek and feta tart with a glass of unoaked
chardonnay at the end of the business day. (Sabrina matches
her meals with wine for a fee.) Two years in business, and she's
making over $45,000 a year after expenses. A step up from
her base salary at the restaurant.*

Self-employment. Whether you've been let go at work like
Sabrina, or want to be your own boss like Keri from the beginning of this chapter, self-employment is hands-down one of
the most exciting and challenging ways to make a buck. (Or a
million of them.)

That's part of the reason why one in 10 women in Canada
is self-employed, according to data by Statistics Canada. By
trading in reserved parking spots at work for their own home's
driveway, women are finding ways to make work match their
lifestyles and current ambitions.

Not that the picture is entirely rosy, especially when you
consider that self-employed women with unincorporated
businesses are nearly half as likely to earn over $20,000 per
year compared to men, especially in rural areas and small
towns. What's more, in most provinces and territories, self-
employed Canadians don't qualify for government benefits
and insurance programs such as disability, maternity or parental leave, employment insurance, and pension programs.

But let's back up for a moment. Yes, as a whole, self-
employed women make less than men. But that lacklustre pay
can be partially attributed to women who make the choice
to work part-time. Indeed, many women choose the self-
employment route so they can take care of kids, check in on
elderly parents, or pursue other passions.

Of course qualifying for government cash would be ideal,
but remember, when you work for yourself, you're writing off
expenses to pay less tax. Knowing this, Sabrina takes some of
the money that would normally go to taxes and she builds a
hefty emergency fund and pours as much as she can into an
RRSP. In short, she not only runs her business, she runs her
finances too.

If you think you might have what it takes to be your own boss, here are a few questions to ask yourself before entering the ranks of the successfully self-employed:

Q: *Will my business make money? Will I be successful?*

A: *That depends on a few factors ranging from how much experience you already have, to whether or not you have a name in the industry or any networking connections, to how saturated the market is. Even if all the stars align, it can still be a tough slog at first. (But don't give up. We believe in you!)*

Q: *Can I handle running a business if I'm used to working for a big corporation?*

A: *Great question. There's definitely a culture shift when you leave an employer behind to go solo. Performing routine office jobs takes some getting used to after fleeing the world of assistants and support staff who take care of financial and administrative tasks. So don't be surprised if at first you find yourself needing a contract and saying, "How do I write that?"*

Q: *How much money do I need to get started?*

A: *As much as you can possibly stockpile, although the actual amount varies depending on whether your business requires a lot of start-up capital to buy equipment or supplies and how much money you need to live on until the first cheque arrives. Aim for six months' worth of living expenses if you can swing it.*

Still have questions about running your own business? Hop online and visit Canadabusiness.gc.ca (a government information service for businesses and start-up entrepreneurs in Canada); Cawee.net (Canadian Association of Women Executives and Entrepreneurs); Canadianbusiness.com (Canadian Business Online, which has an Entrepreneur section); Cdnbizwomen.com (Canadian Women's Business Network); or other local small business groups in your area.

And don't forget industry associations. They'll have even more specific information.

YOU'RE READY

There. You did it. You negotiated yourself a 19 percent pay increase and convinced the boss to let you leave early on Tuesdays to take a class. Or maybe you networked your way into a new career, or decided to give it all up to go the freelance route. Whatever your story, you are now ready—and have the time you need—to crank it up so your earnings give you the life you want. Remember that magic wand?

Over the next three chapters, we're going to map out a plan to help you spend smart, save more, and give debt a run for its money. We're also going to delve into stocks, bonds, mutual funds, and more while helping you find your footing in all things related to investing. It's going to be fun. We'll do our best to make it simple. And by the time we start tackling taxes, mortgages, wills, and pre-nups in later chapters, if by chance you're at a restaurant with friends and somebody pipes up with, "I just don't understand money!" you'll be able to look her right in the eye and say, "Then let me tell you about it."

Chapter 2
SPEND
LIKE
A PRO

••

Time to fess up. Kristin, a 42-year-old law clerk in Moncton, New Brunswick, isn't concerned about making more money. No. She just wishes she knew how to spend what she does have a bit smarter. Not that she takes expensive vacations (often) or splurges on pricey lipstick (much), but she just can't shake the feeling that finding ways to save a few bucks seems like too much work for too little gain.

But it isn't until Kristin visits her best friend's house that she's able to quantify how much she has been squandering both her money and her opportunities. Her pal Veronica bought a new mattress set right after Kristin decided to trade hers in.

"Amazingly, we chose the exact same model from the exact same mattress chain store," says Kristin. "But I couldn't believe the price she paid for hers. Four hundred dollars less than I did. They even threw in a couple of free pillows! At first I was jealous, then I just got angry—at myself."

I T'S NOT THAT KRISTIN IS MISSING A SMART SHOPPING gene or is keen to throw her money away, but how do you explain a chequing account that always seems to dip into the red despite a good income? Something has to change.

The beauty of spending less is that you get to do more with what you have. Yes, you could work harder or work longer hours to make that cash; or, you could take 15 seconds and ask for a discount on that pair of boots with a tiny flaw and score $20 off. Do the math. Those 15 seconds are probably the most lucrative you'll have all day.

Curiosity piqued?

Attention shoppers: keep reading to find out how to stick to a budget, pay bills on time, haggle like it's nobody's business, and turn the dollars you spend into cents you save—so they can grow over time.

MAKE A BUDGET

Listening to her now, you would never know that Katrina Carroll-Foster ever worried about paying her bills. The thirty-something Vancouverite, who works in marketing for an upscale hotel chain, throws around terms like "self-directed RRSP account" and "leveraging my mortgage" like a born financial whiz.

But just a few years ago, Katrina was sinking in a swamp of debt. She tried to knock down the amount of money she owed, throwing $500 at her bills from every paycheque, but the payments hardly made a dent in her $10,000 debt.

Katrina kept spending too. "You're thinking, 'Oh well. If I drop another few hundred, it doesn't matter. It's just tacked on to this enormous debt,' " she admits. Finally, after watching her first RRSP double in value, Katrina realized what compound interest could do when it actually worked in her favour. It was time to take an unflinching look at her money, make a budget—the dreaded monthly plan for spending and saving based on income and costs—and stick with it.

Budget. Does the word make you squirm? A lot of people feel that way. Who wants to feel like someone else—or something else—is telling us how to spend our money? But here's a secret: if you work at it, budgeting can be a crucial first step to solvency. (If it helps, erase "budget" from your personal lexicon and replace it with "spending plan." There. Feel better?)

Whatever you decide to call it, the budget can be as simple as you need it to be. In fact, for most people, straightforward is the way to go. Detailed or not, a budget generally involves just four steps:

1. Identify your income.

2. Figure out how you're spending your money now.

3. Evaluate that spending and come up with goals for saving.

4. Keep tracking expenses and stay within your guidelines.

IDENTIFY YOUR INCOME

This is the easiest stage of the process. Jot down everything you earn per month and per year. Start with your wages, but don't forget to include other streams of cash coming in such as child support, job bonuses, gifts, and rental income. If you tend to receive money in one lump sum annually, divide the amount by 12 to get your monthly total. For more ideas, use the "How much money do I make?" worksheet on page 50.

FIGURE OUT HOW YOU'RE SPENDING YOUR MONEY NOW

Before tracking and recording what you spend, take a stab and guess. You probably already know what the monthly mortgage is, or how far you need to reach into your pocket to pay for utilities. But what about all of those dinners out, mani-pedis, or trips to the liquor store? Write in your speculations under the "Monthly amount" column of the "What should I budget for?" worksheet on page 51.

Now, to track your current spending, first gather up all your routine expenses from the last few months. Think telephone bills, hydro, auto insurance, child care, and anything else you pay regularly. Then, collect your variable expenses such as dry cleaning or coffee on the way to work. Some people like to write these amounts into a notebook, use a mobile app such as MyExpense Tracker or PocketKeeper, or punch them into the computer at the end of the day. Others grab bills and receipts and stuff them into an envelope to be tallied at the end of the month. Just don't change your spending habits yet. Be Zen about it: simply observe.

At the end of the month (or as you go, if you decide to use personal finance software), sort by type of expense and add everything. Write each final tally in the "Actual amount" column of the "What should I budget for?" worksheet.

All this tracking and calculating can seem like drudgery, but it has to be done, says Amanda Mills, a financial therapist in Toronto and owner of Loose Change, a company that helps people tackle their emotional bugaboos about money. "People try to make a plan without knowing what they did last year and they can't stick to it," she says. "Making a budget without knowing where you actually sit is tricky. It's almost useless, actually."

EVALUATE SPENDING AND COME UP WITH GOALS FOR SAVING

After tracking, evaluate the results: how does your spending compare to your earnings? If you're still in the black, maybe you just need to make a few changes. If you're spending more than you earn and dipping into credit to make up the difference, however, it's time for a financial shakedown.

What are you spending and why? Is there anything you would like to spend more money on? Is there anything you can spend less money on? As you probably discovered when comparing your "Monthly amount" with your "Actual amount" columns, most people severely underestimate what they spend on items such as groceries, a night's entertainment, lunch at the food court during the workweek, or clothes for the family. Can you shop at a less expensive grocery store? Maybe take in a movie at a second-run cinema instead of the multiplex? Or perhaps it's time to brown bag it twice a week.

If you want to take this spending plan one step further, look at some of the small nonessential purchases you make each month and log them in to the "How the little things add up" worksheet on page 54. A happy-hour glass of wine each Friday after work might only cost you $9 with tip each week, but over a full year, you're paying $468. Now maybe that's okay with you because that glass of wine is worth more than the drink itself. Maybe you look forward to unwinding with colleagues and friends at the end of the week and the $468 keeps you sane year-round. But you need to look at what its purely monetary value is too. Added up, that money is enough to pay for a weekend getaway to wine country.

So tracking and evaluating expenditures also serves another purpose. When people think about how much money they spend as they're spending it, they gradually and naturally start to shift away from buying things they want, toward buying things they need (or *really* want). A few years ago Mills herself started tracking how much money she was spending on lattes and discovered that the figure was coming in at $300 a month, or $3,600 a year. Simply by evaluating one expense, Mills realized she could buy a machine to make her lattes at the office and save a lot of money.

KEEP TRACKING EXPENSES AND STAY WITHIN YOUR GUIDELINES

The last step to becoming budget-wise is the most difficult: follow your plan. If you're sick of tracking expenses after one month, take a break and dive into slashing your spending. (You'll find some fantastic ways to slice and dice your spending later in this chapter.) It can be as complicated as switching to a bank that uses the average daily balance method for calculating minimum balance and interest, or as simple as sticking money in a jar or envelope. The latter system, by the way, is as easy as it gets. After determining how much money you're spending, pinpoint the places you can cut back—no more big splurges at the grocery store, for instance—and stuff the correlating amount of cash into a jar.

If, however, you actually enjoy tracking everything you buy, by all means keep at it. By tracking over the course of a few months, you'll have a chance to see where you tend to fall down and research ways to pick your spending habits back up again. Reuse the "What should I budget for?" worksheet on page 51. But this time, take what you learned from the previous months to plan next month's budget, and then compare it to what you actually end up spending. Then use that information to plan for the following month. Over time, you'll see real results—your estimated budget and your actual budget will start to look a lot more alike.

One last word of advice: don't be too hard on yourself. Budgeting isn't about being punitive or placing blame (this is especially important when you're going through the process with a husband or partner). It's about making informed decisions. Besides, that daily chocolate bar might be giving you as much pleasure as your Aunt Marla's season tickets to the opera give her.

Your budget has to make sense to you.

SPEND IT SMART!

"Help! My budget doesn't work!" Sound like you? Relax. Budgets are meant to be tweaked and changed to reflect your lifestyle and personality. Here are a few tips to get back on track:

- Maybe the method is the madness. If you can't stand tracking expenses using a notebook and pen, try collecting receipts instead. If you hate typing them into Microsoft Money or Quicken, maybe your kids will do it for a small fee.

- You really want that electric sandwich grill (and maybe three more because they're such a deal). Before you buy, picture the prospective purchase in your house—collecting dust. That's probably what it will be doing in a couple of weeks. Do you still want it?

- Use a checklist when you go grocery shopping, but allow yourself one or two surprise purchases. Restrictive budgeting is like restrictive dieting. Neither work.

- Plan for budget busters. Did you anticipate spending on municipal house taxes? Holiday gift giving? Your daughter's dental work? Don't forget to include sporadic expenses in the budget or you'll be pulling out the credit card instead.

- If nothing is working or you're dealing with a lot of personal debt, call a financial advisor. And don't forget not-for-profit credit counselling agencies. Find your local branch at Creditcounsellingcanada.ca. ▪

HOW MUCH MONEY DO I MAKE?

Worksheet No. 1

Income	Annual amount	Monthly amount
Wages: yours, after taxes	$	$
Wages: others' in the home, after taxes	$	$
Paid overtime	$	$
Job bonuses	$	$
Child support	$	$
Earned interest and dividends on investments or savings	$	$
Government child benefits	$	$
Pension and social security benefits	$	$
Tax refunds	$	$
Small business income	$	$
Rental income	$	$
Gifts	$	$
Other	$	$
Total Income	$	$

WHAT SHOULD I BUDGET FOR?

Worksheet No. 2

Expenses	Monthly amount	Actual amount
Mortgages or rent	$	$
Home repairs and upgrades	$	$
Home and contents insurance	$	$
Home taxes (divide annual amount by 12)	$	$
Vehicle(s) lease or loan payment	$	$
Car sharing fees (Zipcar, Co-operative Auto Network, etc.)	$	$
Auto insurance premiums	$	$
Gas	$	$
Car repairs	$	$
Other transportation fees: bus or subway fare, commuter rail passes, etc.	$	$
Utilities: electricity	$	$
Utilities: gas/heating oil	$	$
Water	$	$
Land line telephone: basic service long distance other service fees	$	$
Internet	$	$

▶▶

Expenses	Monthly amount	Actual amount
Cellphone: basic service roaming fees data (email, text, etc.) fees other service fees	$	$
Cable or satellite TV: basic service extra service fees	$	$
Groceries	$	$
Alcohol	$	$
Snacks, coffee, drinks on the run	$	$
Restaurant meals and takeout	$	$
Child care	$	$
Alimony	$	$
Child support or other support to family members	$	$
Clothing	$	$
Dry cleaning bills	$	$
Pet expenses	$	$
Computer lease fees	$	$
Health insurance	$	$
Dentist bills	$	$
Prescription medications	$	$
Other medical expenses (contact lenses, vitamins, etc.)	$	$
Charitable donations	$	$
Loan payments (other than mortgage or auto)	$	$
Credit card payments	$	$
RRSP contribution	$	$
RESP contribution	$	$
Pension contribution	$	$

►►

Expenses	Monthly amount	Actual amount
Emergency fund contribution	$	$
Home business expenses (pens, paper, printer cartridges, extra phone line, etc.)	$	$
Union or professional association dues	$	$
Personal expenses (toiletries, manicures, etc.)	$	$
Entertainment fees	$	$
Classes	$	$
Reading material	$	$
Hobbies	$	$
Sports-related fees (gym memberships, yoga classes)	$	$
Vacation fund	$	$
Religious contributions	$	$
Gifts (birthdays, weddings, holidays, etc.)	$	$
Other	$	$
Total Expenses	$	$

Compare income and expenses

Monthly Income (total from "How much money do I make?" worksheet): $_____

Monthly Expenses (total from "What should I budget for?" worksheet): $_____

Subtract expenses from income and list amount difference here: $_____

HOW THE LITTLE THINGS ADD UP

Only you know how you spend your discretionary dollars, so consider this table a sample template that you can use to create a spreadsheet specific to your own spending habits.

Worksheet No. 3

What you bought	What you paid	Cost per month	Cost per year
Lattes at work (example: 2 per workday for 21 days)	$3.26 × 2	$136.92	$1,643.04
New clothes	$	$	$
Eating out	$	$	$
Snacks and runs to the convenience store	$	$	$
Lottery tickets	$	$	$
Movies	$	$	$
CDs or music downloads	$	$	$
Gifts	$	$	$
Other	$	$	$
Total	$	$	$

SKILLS TO PAY THE BILLS

Sophie, a professional wedding planner in Ottawa and mom of three, hates paying bills. No, let's rephrase that. She hates the stress she feels when she's late paying them. Telephone, cellphone, credit cards, hydro, gas, water, taxes—who can keep up with it all? Feeling overwhelmed by the stack cramming her mailbox each month, not to mention all of her other responsibilities, Sophie does what a lot of busy women find themselves doing: throwing bills in a pile and promptly forgetting about them until—oops—they're racking up late fees.

"I just found a bill I was four months late paying and I had no idea. I'm amazed no one cut off my service," she says.

That bill, thankfully, was a wake-up call. Sophie got serious about making payments on time. She and her husband sat down with their monthly invoices, a calculator, a calendar, and some paper and pens, and mapped out a plan to make bill paying automatic and, dare we say it, painless.

Maybe, like Sophie, you periodically forget to pay the piper (or the taxman, or the credit card collector) or even lose an important bill. For mere monetary mortals, overdue bills are often chalked up to living harried lives in which anything that can be put off until tomorrow slides onto the back burner for weeks or months instead. (Remember how long it took you to draw up a budget?)

But there are some major upsides to paying your bills on time. Your credit score remains higher so every time you apply for a loan, mortgage, or insurance you'll get a better rate. Not only that, but forget to pay credit card bills and you might as well stand up and say, "Come on. Hike my interest rate. And while you're at it, why don't you charge me a $25 late fee?"

It's true. Many credit card offers that encourage us to transfer our outstanding balance from a higher rate card to a lower one boast extremely competitive interest rates in the neighbourhood of 3.9 to 5.9 percent. But if you miss a payment? That "introductory" rate is gone and you're back to paying 18 or 22 percent in interest. Even rates that are already in the nosebleed section can be shot into the stratosphere in response to late payments.

That's the bad news. The good news is that there is a smart, simple way to ditch disorganization, keep track of bills, pay them on time, and reap the financial rewards.

KEEP IT TOGETHER

Find a place in your house and designate it "Bill Central." Maybe it's your desk, a spot on your kitchen counter, or a hanging file on the wall beside the front door. Wherever it is, make sure it's easy to access and stocked with your cheque-book, envelopes, stamps, pens, calculator, stapler, and return address labels. You'll also want a larger envelope to keep your bills in. On it, write "Pay Me" or "Bills to be Paid," or whatever will draw your attention. Once safely inside, bills are less likely to go missing.

WRITE IT OUT

This step is simple. Make a list of all your bills. By taking the time to write down every company you owe money to, you'll have a big picture view of where that dough needs to go.

CHOOSE YOUR DAYS

Next, choose two days every month to pay bills. With grace periods becoming shorter and shorter, paying bills more often means you're much more likely to pay before the deadline passes. Just remember to consider your work payment cycle. If you're paid on the 15th and 30th of every month, setting your bill payment dates is easy. But if you're paid more sporadic-ally, you'll have to pull out the calendar and figure out which days will work best for you. Whichever dates you choose, write "PAY BILLS" in big letters on the calendar or type them in all caps into your electronic day planner. Better still, schedule an electronic reminder to pop up on your computer the day pay-ment is due.

WHEN THE BILLS COME IN

Whether the bills land in your mailbox or your inbox when they arrive, look them over to make sure you haven't been overcharged. Inaccuracies happen more often than you might expect. If everything looks kosher, stick them in your Pay Me file. When the pay date rolls around, pay the bills and record information about each transaction on your copy of the invoice and place it in a bills-paid file. Or, if you prefer to keep all like invoices filed together for future reference (say, all of your paid hydro bills in one file and all of your MasterCard invoices in another), mark the following on each one before filing them away:

1. Date paid

2. Amount paid

3. Cheque number or online transaction number

PAY BILLS WITH HIGH INTEREST RATES AND LATE FEES FIRST

Hmm. Bill A or Bill B? If you're forced to pick and choose which bill to pay first, always go with the ones that either charge you a late payment fee or a high interest rate. Not only are you trying to pay your bills on time, but you're also trying to pay less overall.

GO ONLINE

Just a few years ago most of us were waiting for bills to come in the mail and sending cheques out that way too. But now at least six out of 10 Canadians fire up their computers to pay bills online. If you aren't already doing it, just call your financial institution, answer a few questions, and soon you'll have access to your account online day and night. (The service also allows you to pay bills by phone.) Online bill paying is beyond simple. Log in, pay up, and record the details. That's it. What's more, the bank keeps a record of your payments. Or you could go one step further and sign up for epost, a free online service from Canada Post that sends your e-bills to one secure virtual location and lets you pay them there. Visit Epost.ca.

MAKE IT AUTOMATIC

Never miss a payment again! At least that's the goal if you set up pre-authorized payments for recurring bills like the mortgage, telephone, or hydro. The upside is you'll eliminate late fees no matter what. The downside is that if you're running close to the wire each month and the gas bill skyrockets in January, or someone in your house yakked it up with a friend in Australia causing the telephone invoice to jump, you might find yourself in the red and paying overdraft or NSF fees instead. Use this option only for bills with predictable monthly rates or if you have ample cash flow.

IF YOU MISS A PAYMENT

Hospital stays, vacations, and simple forgetfulness. Even those with good habits drop the ball sometimes. But is there anything you can do if you happen to miss a payment? Sure. Don't be afraid to negotiate. For example, if your card-issuing bank charges you a credit card late fee, but you usually pay on time, call and ask them to waive it. Many banks will relinquish late fees at least once for customers with excellent payment records. Some service companies do too.

JUST DO IT

Finally, we might as well just say it—some people dread paying bills and will do almost anything to avoid opening envelopes. If this sounds like you, take a moment and ask yourself why. Are you actually living beyond your means and those cold, hard numbers drive that fact home with a terrifying thud? Or maybe you're self-employed and you worry that if you pay your bills now, you might not have enough money in your bank account before the next client's cheque arrives. Whatever is holding you back from making payments, just remember that doing nothing will make your anxiety much worse. Taking action—paying your bills—puts you on a feel-good path to financial freedom. So go for it.

SPEND IT SMART!

You've just stumbled in the door from work, the dog needs to be let outside, and the kids' pleas for a snack 20 minutes before dinnertime are about to catapult you over the edge.

Sort through that new stack of bills sitting on the counter pronto? Yeah right.

We all know it's a good idea to tackle bills as soon as they land in the mailbox, but sometimes life makes that worthy goal seem unlikely. So here's an idea: instead of allowing paper bills to collect with the promise to deal with them later, tack a piece of paper on the kitchen wall where you'll see it, rip envelopes open when bills arrive, and *immediately* write down the name of whom you owe and the payment due date on the sheet. This takes a minute, tops. Then, if you don't even have time to sort, just chuck the bills into your big holding envelope. Every time a new bill comes in, mark down the info. Every time a bill is paid, cross it off the list.

If the writing is quite literally on the wall, you'll be more likely to remember to pay up and avoid costly late fees later. ■

EVERY CENT COUNTS, COUNT EVERY CENT

Now the fun part: spending money the smart way.

A couple of minutes before bed, you pop onto the computer, pay your bills, recheck your bank balance online and—gasp—there are hundreds of extra dollars just sitting there! Mistake?

Miracle? Nope. While tracking your spending and examining the results, you've found simple ways to save cash by shaving 20, 50, or even 70 percent off your bank fees, grocery bills, utilities, and even haircuts. And the financial gain you'll now get in just a few short days? Priceless. Here are some creative ways to cut back *right now*:

AT THE BANK

- Open an account with a bank that has ATMs and branches near home and work to avoid the added cost of visiting an alternate bank's machine out of desperation. Here's the math: if you withdraw $20 from an ATM belonging to another financial institution and it charges you $1.50, you've just paid a 7.5 percent surcharge to access your own money. What's more, your bank may also charge you an out-of-network transaction fee.

- Open an online bank account. Online banks, such as ING DIRECT, don't pay for bricks and mortar so they can pass along savings to you in the form of higher interest rates. Many even boast no fees. (Although read the fine print. Some things, such as extra ATM transactions, you have to pay for.)

- Consider putting your money in credit unions or caisses populaires, which offer many of the same products and services as the big banks. By buying a small share at a credit union, you may be able to take advantage of lower interest credit cards or higher interest savings accounts.

- If you keep a big balance in an interest-bearing account, check if your bank uses the average daily balance method for calculating minimum balance and interest. As long as your average daily balance for the *entire month* is above the minimum you're allowed, you'll be much less likely to be charged a fee if you dip below that. What's more, you'll earn interest on all your money. Other methods of calculating interest can wipe out hundreds of dollars a year worth of interest credited to your account.

CHEAP EATS

- Looking for ways to go green and lower your environmental "cookprint" in the kitchen while cutting the cost of your electricity bill? Replace old appliances such as refrigerators—the kitchen's biggest energy hog, which eats up over 10 percent of the entire home's electricity—with energy-efficient ones (look for the ENERGY STAR label). You'll come out ahead. ENERGY STAR refrigerators, for example, use less than half the electricity of 10-year-old models. And don't forget to set the fridge to its optimum temperature: 3°C.

- Take a cue from the seasons to find ways to cut down on energy use while whipping up dinner. In the summer, replace steak and marinated veggies on the grill for a no-cook green salad with marinated leftover chicken. Cooking a casserole? Forget preheating the oven for 20 minutes while slicing and dicing ingredients. Five minutes should do it. Or steam your dinner vegetables in the microwave and use up to 75 percent less energy than you would on the stove.

- Would you pay someone $80 an hour to grate your cheese? That's what nutrition researchers at Arizona State University in Tempe say you could be forking out if you're buying packages of pre-grated cheese. So, if your priority is saving money over saving time, do the work in your own kitchen. (The researchers also found that it only takes 1½ minutes to grate a pound of cheese by hand.) But cheese isn't the only

DIY food choice. If you love to chow down on roast beef or smoked turkey sandwiches, buy meat ends at the grocery store and slice them at home. You'll be cutting your deli bill in half.

- Switch to a big box or club store, where you'll find great deals if you're buying items in bulk. Split the cost of a membership card (approx. $55) with a friend and save even more if you shop together and divide the bulk items (and the bill) in half. Just remember to walk into the store with a firm list in hand, and stick to it, or you could come home with a new trampoline for the kids and a new hole in your wallet.

- If shopping at a big box store makes you break out in hives, visit your local farmer during the harvest season. Buying directly from a grower at a farmers' market is often cheaper than going to the grocery store (for example, you could pay about 75 cents for a head of organic lettuce compared to $1.50 at the supermarket). You can save even more if you find a farmer who will sell you second-grade produce. No, we're not encouraging you to shell out for mouldy tomatoes. The fruits and veggies taste just fine. Many organic farmers toss one-third of their crop because markets often prohibit them from selling cosmetically imperfect produce. By offering to buy misshapen cukes and apples, you'll save green on your greens.

- Do you usually give in to impulse buys? Bring just enough cash to cover what's on your list. Up to 50 percent of what we end up carting home from the grocery store probably wasn't on our original shopping lists, says Pat Foran, author of *Canadian Consumer Alert: 101 Ways to Protect Yourself and Your Money*.

- With grocery prices climbing, it's time to stop worrying about looking cheap at the checkout counter and give the old clip-and-save a go. An average four-person family can save between 10 and 20 percent off its annual grocery bill if it uses coupons. Just remember the one chief rule of coupon clippers: don't buy a product simply because you can get a deal. If you weren't going to buy it anyway, you're not saving money, you're spending money.

- Do you find yourself throwing out a crisper's worth of limp carrots and slimy lettuce come garbage day? We often buy so much food that we forget what we have. But you're not the only one. A study from Statistics Canada found that in 2007 nearly 40 percent of our food supply was wasted by households, restaurants, and supermarkets. Here's an idea: put off grocery shopping one week every month so you can eat up what you've already got and you'll save hundreds of dollars each year.

BE ENERGY SMART

- Reduce your energy bills by using your air conditioner only on the days that you really need it instead of leaving it on all summer. Or buy a programmable thermostat (about $70) and set it so the air conditioner is off during the day and clicks on an hour before everyone comes home. You'll still be walking into a cool house without paying a cool wad of cash. In winter, set the thermostat a few degrees lower during the day and at bedtime. You can save about two percent of your heating and cooling costs for every degree Celsius lowered or raised.

- Hang your clothes to dry. Especially in the winter, it's a good way to humidify a dry house.

- Shrink your family heating and cooling bill further by making a few changes around the house. Install ceiling fans, plant shade trees beside the house, and put up heat-reflective PVC vertical blinds. And don't forget to insulate. By insulating and drywalling the basement and attic—the two places that tend to lose the most heat in winter—you'll save about five to 10 percent of your heating and cooling costs.

- Close your fireplace damper to keep cooling costs down in summer. If you don't use the fireplace often, Natural Resources Canada suggests plugging the chamber with a cloth-covered board. (Just remember to remove it before lighting the first fire of the season!)

- Turn them off! Flick off the pilot light on your gas furnace during the spring and summer months. You'll hack $200 off your heating tab. Or switch off the air conditioner breaker on your electrical panel when summer is over. Leaving it on all winter means you're heating oil in the outside cooling unit and throwing away $25.

- Wrap a foil insulation blanket around your hot-water tank (you'll find these at home-improvement stores for about $25). While you're there, pick up some ½ in. (1 cm) thick foam tubing at about $2 per 6 ft. (1.8 m) to cover the water heater's copper and metal hot water pipes. Total savings: up to $200 a year! Or opt for one of the newer tankless heaters that warms water only when needed.

- Ditch your old strings of conventional Christmas lights and light up over the thought of using 90 percent less electricity with new LED lights instead. Even better news? Manufacturers are finally making softer, gentler versions that don't blind you.

- Power down. Turn off your computer when you're not using it. Unplug power eaters such as TVs, DVD players, and stereos when not being used. They draw energy even when they're turned off.

- Laptops and battery chargers eat up a lot of energy. Next time you take the company laptop home to finish a report, charge it at work so you're not picking up the tab.

- If you have a small lawn, sell your gas-guzzling lawn mower and use the money to buy a manual push mower (about $100). Keep the blades sharp and you'll hardly notice a difference—and you'll get a nice little workout too.

STREAMLINE YOUR MONEY

- Call your credit card-issuing bank and ask for a rate reduction. Take any of your credit cards that are carrying a balance, flip them over, and call the number on the back. Say that you want them to reduce your interest rate or you'll take your business elsewhere. If the first person you talk to won't do it, politely and firmly ask to talk to a supervisor. If you have a $5,000 balance, even a three percent rate reduction saves you $150 a year.

- Shop around for the best service fees. If your bank charges you $12.50 each month in account fees, plus dings you $1 for every ATM withdrawal or bill payment after your 20-transaction limit (and let's face it, is that limit ever enough?), it's time to reassess options. Move your money to something like a no-fee account offered by the grocery-store-based bank, and you can save $10, $15, or even $30 in fees per month with free cheques, bill payments, and *Interac* direct purchases.

- Pay your mortgage every two weeks instead of monthly. Here's why: if you pay about $350 biweekly instead of $700 monthly on a $100,000 mortgage, you'll save almost $24,000 in interest over 25 years, assuming a fixed seven percent interest rate. And don't forget to bump up your mortgage payments every time you get a raise. Paying just $20 a week extra over five years could chop $5,000 off your mortgage over the long haul.

- Who wouldn't love to earn tax-free cash? Look for tax-free savings accounts that allow customers to deposit up to $5,000 each year. The interest earned is yours, tax-free. For instance, if you earned 2.7 percent interest on $5,000, the $135 in interest that year wouldn't be subject to tax—saving you $19. This may not seem like much at first, but the savings will compound nicely over the long haul.

- When was the last time you thought about your insurance rates? Check out InsuranceHotline.com and compare rates for the same coverage. Did you find a company willing to give you a better deal? If you decide to make the switch before the renewal date with your current company rolls around, make sure you won't incur a penalty by making the leap early.

CAR-FRIENDLY SAVINGS

- Take care of your vehicle and you'll save megabucks on costly repairs down the road. So keep your oil clean—it's what keeps your engine humming. Getting a $40 oil-and-filter change every 5,000 km costs much less than replacing a $4,000 engine someday. And don't forget to have the entire vehicle rust proofed to prevent brake lines and other parts from corroding. Regular car washes also help keep rust at bay.

- Check your tires' air pressure at least once a month. With proper pressure, you can increase the life of your tires by as much as 15 percent and boost fuel efficiency too. On new cars, you'll find the automaker's recommended pressure on the driver's doorjamb. On older cars it can be on the trunk lid, fuel door, glove box, centre console lid, passenger's doorjamb, or in your owner's manual.

- Check your car's air filter monthly. A dirty filter shortens the engine's life and reduces gas mileage up to 10 percent. Clean the filter by removing it and blowing it with an air hose.

- When hitting the pump, don't use a higher octane gas than your owner's manual recommends. For most cars, premium gasoline, which costs 10 to 15 percent more than regular, offers no benefit. And forget "topping up the tank" too. Some of the gas may end up overflowing when it expands in the heat or if you park on a hill. The result? Money down the sewer.

GET A HEALTH-CARE OVERHAUL

- It's time to stop watching your hard-earned money go up in smoke. Not only does smoking kill, it also puts a serious dent in the wallet. A pack-a-day habit may cost you up to $3,650 every year. Smokers also pay up to 50 percent more for life insurance. Quit now and ask about a non-smoker's discount for contents and home insurance. To qualify, all members of the household must be non-smokers and visitors will have to light up outside.

- You had a baby a couple of weeks ago and a bill from the hospital lands in the mailbox demanding you pay an extra $125 because the insurance company doesn't cover upgrades to a private room. The thing is, there were no other beds available that day. Should

you pay up? Not so fast. Give your hospital's billing
department a call first and plead your case. Experts
say many hospital bills contain overcharges and
errors, but if you don't point them out, you'll be stuck
delivering a wad of bills.

THE GREAT CANADIAN SHOP CHOP

- If you're on the petite side, hit the same clothing
  stores that your kids frequent. By doing this, that
  pair of leggings, for instance, will look identical, be
  at least a third cheaper, and, best yet, they'll actually
  fit you.

- Tired of wearing the same old clothes but can't
  stomach the thought of paying for a new wardrobe?
  Instead of buying a new blouse for work, consider
  swapping with friends. Swap events, also called
  swishing, let pals gather together to trade good
  clothing they don't wear anymore. Consignment
  stores also hold swishing parties.

- Maintain your 'do without breaking the bank.
  Instead of paying for a full head of highlights every
  time you get a haircut, ask your stylist for root touch-
  ups instead. Or if your hair is on the longer side and
  you colour, chop the ends every *other* time you pay
  to hide your greys. You can end up saving over $200
  each year.

- Clip online coupons. Flipping through newspaper
  flyers to be in the know about great deals is old
  school. There are endless online resources that make
  bargain hunting effortless. To shop around virtually,
  simply visit Flyerland.ca and type your city into the
  database. Print off the coupons and you can save on
  everything from groceries to department store goods.
  Or check out Smartcanucks.ca, Canadianfreestuff.ca,
  Save.ca, and Redflagdeals.com for other handy
  Canadian deals.

SPEND IT SMART!

Here's one more way to save money that you'd probably never think of: haggling. That's right. Asking a sales clerk or customer rep to give you the same goods for less.

Try these lines and strategies to sway a salesperson:

- **"Can you beat this price?"** Ask different vendors their price for the same merchandise or service. Once you have the range, go back to the company you want to buy from and ask them to beat the lowest price.
- **"Hmmm."** Use silence as a weapon. If the salesperson offers you a deal you're not happy with, say nothing and wait. This works well if you're on the fence and the clerk wants to make the sale.
- **"I only have X dollars to spend."** Even if you're willing to pay more, go in claiming you have only so much money on reserve. If you have to negotiate up a little, it's not the end of the world and everyone feels they're a winner.
- **"Is it almost closing time?"** Never try haggling on days when business is booming. Try a Tuesday evening or Thursday morning. Particularly if you show up at the end of the day, salespeople will often be more open to striking a deal.

OWN OR LEASE A CAR?

With all of that found money hanging around in your bank account, you might be tempted to live life in the fast lane and spend some of it on a new car. You're driving an ancient electric blue Pontiac Sunfire with a cracked windshield and missing mirror and it's no longer safe. You've been saving up for that sweet little Miata convertible and it's time for a test drive. You just had baby number three and a minivan is in her future . . . and yours.

Whatever car you choose, you'll need to decide whether it makes sense to lease or buy it new. Considering transportation is typically the second or third biggest expense you'll carry, think it through before signing anything.

DRIVING POINTS

Let's start with the obvious: if you buy a car you own it outright. But if you decide to lease, your lessor (usually a credit company affiliated with the car manufacturer) owns your ride and, in essence, you're paying them to drive the car. The lessor also charges you interest, usually referred to as the lease rate. So what's the advantage to leasing? Monthly payments. When you lease a vehicle, the amount of money you pay each month may be less than what you would pay if you bought the car. The hitch is that at the end of the lease, you must either return the car and walk away, or pay a "buyback" fee, which reflects the value of the car, to purchase it.

KEEP IT UP

You know how your mother taught you to return whatever you borrowed in the same condition it came to you in? The same applies to a leased car. So no custom paint jobs, stay away from bumper stickers that rip the finish, and stick to the maintenance schedule the seller gives you. To avoid disagreements, have an independent inspection done before returning the car.

IF YOU DRIVE A LOT

Do you take long road trips? Is your commute a killer? Whether you buy or lease, the more mileage on the car, the faster it depreciates in value. If you own the car, it simply means you will sell it at a lower price when the time comes. But if you lease the car, you may have to pay extra for those miles through the company's mileage allowance plans, usually offered at 80,000 km, 100,000 km and 120,000 km over four years. Still think that's not enough? Purchase additional kilometres to avoid paying for costly clicks if you go over your limit.

TIME TO BAIL

The time has come to sell the car you own. You can, as long as you pay your car loan back in full. If you want to break a lease, however, you will have to pay all of your remaining lease payments or risk accruing big penalties, not to mention a black mark on your credit report. Try subleasing or transferring your lease first.

SO . . . BUY OR LEASE?

That depends. If you have the money to make bigger payments and you plan on keeping the vehicle for a long time, it makes better financial sense to buy the car. You're building up equity and, after interest is taken in to account, it's cheaper than leasing over the long haul.

But let's say you're just out of school, or you've just gone back to work after a hiatus, or you're picking yourself up after a divorce and money is in short supply. Leasing might make sense to you right now since the payments are often lower and you'll avoid nasty maintenance surprises that afflict older cars. And here's one more reason why someone might choose lease over ownership: anyone with sky-high debt and high interest fees can take the money saved by leasing a car over the short term and use it to pay off their debt.

Or opt for possibly the most financially prudent choice of all: buy used and let someone else pay for the costly depreciation in those first three or four years. You'll pay lease-worthy prices and own the car in the end. Plus, if you drive it until it eventually dies, you could end up with cheap wheels for the last few years before that happens. Years you can spend socking money away in RRSPs or building up your child's education fund. (Just remember frequent tune-ups to avoid breakdowns at the side of the road with said child.) In short you'll be laughing, while driving, all the way to the bank.

Here are a few pros and cons you'll want to consider before buying a used car off the lot:

The pros:

- The price is lower than a comparable new car.

- Ownership expenses such as collision insurance and taxes are lower. (If you decide to buy an extended warranty for your used vehicle, read the fine print and do all maintenance required or your claim could be rejected.)

- You might get a better-equipped vehicle than you'd be able to afford new.

- With improved rust-proofing and exhaust technology, used cars are now considered much more reliable than they were in the past.

- You'll typically pay less to insure a used vehicle than a new version of the same vehicle.

The cons:

- A used car is either close to coming off warranty or already off it.

- You could buy a lemon. Even a model known for its reliability can be a risky proposition if a previous owner abused it or it was in a collision and the owner does not come clean. (To avoid the problem, have it thoroughly inspected by a qualified mechanic.)

- Buying a used car means you might not have the latest safety features such as electronic stability control (ESC), curtain air bags, or the LATCH child safety seat anchoring system.

COMPLAIN AND GET YOUR MONEY BACK

So you succumbed to an urge to splurge, hit the sale racks, asked for a few extra dollars off for a missing button, and now you're carrying home bags of clothes and a belt you've been coveting for months. But there's a problem in pecuniary paradise. After two days of wear, that belt's buckle has snapped, and while you followed the washing instructions to the letter, your new sweater would barely fit a Chihuahua. It feels like your hard-earned money is now floating down the drain with the wash water. What can you do?

The bad news is you don't always have the automatic right to take it back for a full refund or exchange. According to the Canadian Council of Better Business Bureaus, unless the store has agreed to offer refunds and exchanges upfront, they're under no obligation to give you your money back.

But, there's good news too. If you're polite yet firm and play by the rules, you might just get the results you're after.

READ THE PAPERWORK

Know what you're entitled to as a customer. It's a good idea to read all of your paperwork—receipts, warranties—before heading back to the store. (So keep track of your receipts and store them in a receipt folder beside your bills to keep them from going AWOL.) Knowing the laws of your province, as they pertain to shoddy goods and unsatisfactory service, is also your responsibility. For instance, in Ontario, a consumer has the right to cancel a sales contract and obtain a full refund if a product is not delivered within 30 days of the promised delivery date. Want to know more? Visit Consumerinformation.ca, a web portal of consumer information from the federal Office of Consumer Affairs.

ACT FAST AND FOLLOW THE RULES

When a store says you have 14 days to return an item, honour the rule. You'll have a much tougher time making a trade or getting a refund if you wait until day 17. And play nice. Start your complaint process with the front-line customer sales rep and give her time to make things right. If she can't or won't help, that's when you talk to the manager. If you're not getting anywhere with her either, go up the chain and take your complaint to head office.

WRITE A LETTER

Whether you email it or visit the merchant's website to send a complaint via an online form, writing a letter not only feels good, it's also your record of correspondence. Include specific details, the date of purchase, and names of staff if applicable. Then state that you are entitled to a refund under consumer law (if that is indeed the case) and spell out when you expect to hear back. Fourteen days is usually enough. If you are a frequent buyer, spell that out too. Companies want to keep their best customers from walking.

STAY CALM

If you feel yourself getting emotional (after all, who likes to hear the word, "no"?) take a deep breath and keep your cool. It's easy to feel like you're about to snap after being put on hold for the umpteenth time, but you're much more likely to receive a refund if you keep your anger in check. Be firm and direct when explaining your problem to customer service agents. And don't yell or become abusive in any way. That will only get the other person's back up and she'll be much less inclined to find a solution. If confrontations give you hives, write down the points you want to make and stick to the script.

KEEP AN OPEN MIND

You can't always get what you want—but you can accept alternative solutions to your conundrum. If the seller won't give you a full refund, ask what else they can do for you. Maybe you'll end up with a partial refund, credit note, or compensation for repairs.

TAKE IT TO COURT

If nothing else works and you've exhausted all other options, you might consider taking your case to small claims court if you're trying to reclaim at least a few hundred dollars. You won't need a lawyer to argue your case and it won't cost you a fortune either if your claim is under the maximum allowed in your province ($6,000 in New Brunswick or $10,000 in Ontario, for instance). But be forewarned: the court system will never win points for speed and you could end up spending a lot of time going over paperwork. The upside? Especially if you're going up against a larger company, small claims court often seems to side with the consumer.

SPEND IT SMART!

You want to make a consumer complaint but are unsure how to pull it off to get the results you want. Help is here. Visit the Canadian Consumer Information Gateway's Complaint Courier. This online tool helps you prepare your complaint and provides advice on how to complain effectively. Its database even automatically channels complaints to the appropriate agencies. No muss, no fuss.

Visit http://consumerinformation.ca/ and select the "File a Complaint" option. ■

NEXT STOP: DEBT BUSTERS

If you mine these ideas and use them to spend smarter, the extra money in your wallet will amaze you. What's more, once you're on a roll and, say, shredding your own cheese, or haggling for the best deal on a car, it's going to hit you: stretching a dollar is the equivalent of giving yourself a raise! You're not being miserly. You're not being cheap. You're taking control of your money and making it do what it was supposed to be doing all along: paying for daily living expenses *and* helping you live the life you want. And there's even more good news to come. In the next chapter we'll give you a road map to employ incredibly useful strategies to get out of debt, stay out of debt, save face, and save your money too.

Chapter 3
DEBT: KNOW WHAT YOU OWE

· ·

Melissa, an ESL teacher and textbook writer in Vancouver, never meant to fall in love with her credit cards. When she signed up for her first one in university, scooping up a free MP3 player in the process, she hardly gave it a thought. What was one card with a $5.00 limit? Surely she could handle that.

And she did. For the next five or six years, as Melissa's credit limit rose to $1,000, then $3,000, and eventually hit $7,000, she paid her purchases in full each month and mentally patted herself on the back for her fiscally reliable ways. She was even on the road to hacking down her condo's mortgage and paying off her student loan.

But then, slowly, without even realizing it, Melissa started loosening up with her spending. Her best friend suddenly decided to get married down in Aruba and Melissa threw the wedding expenses, resort fees, and plane ticket on a new card she'd signed up for that offered travel points. Then an *inspection revealed her condo's underground parking lot needed crucial structural repairs. The price tag? Over $8,000 for her share of the construction costs.*

She ran out and applied for a line of credit to pay for it.

Soon Melissa found herself signing up for store credit cards, swept up by the promise of saving 20 percent off her new sofa or 30 percent off a winter jacket. And when envelopes began pouring in from credit card companies offering low introductory rates if she moved her current balance to them, she took advantage of those deals too. Unfortunately she also skimmed over the incomprehensible fine print warning that if she bought anything new on the card, the transferred balance would be changed back to the normal 18.5 percent interest rate. Oops.

"For a while there I had 11 credit cards, a mortgage, a line of credit, and some money still outstanding on my student loan. But because I was paying a little bit off them each month, I had no idea how truly in debt I was," she says today. "I was just paying some interest off the top, but little principal."

It wasn't until she sat down one evening to go over the books that it finally hit her: Melissa was in trouble. Some $21,567 worth of trouble.

"I sat there at the table and cried. I was in shock. It was terrible," she says.

But that open window looking on to her financial landscape was also a godsend. The same night, Melissa, cracking open a box of Christmas chocolates to keep her going, worked out a plan to delete her debt in just over four years.

HE DID IT. WANT TO FIND OUT HOW? EVEN IF YOU'RE not up to the eyeballs in debt as Melissa found herself, keep reading because in this chapter we're going to shine light on how debt can sneak up on us when we least expect, what to do if it does, and how to stay out of it in the first place. You'll also discover the difference between good debt (honestly) and bad debt, why it pays to check your credit reports, how to avoid high-risk debt, and how to, gulp, declare bankruptcy. And yes, how to pick yourself up again after the deed is done.

This is what you're *not* going to find on these pages: Doom and gloom. Finger pointing. Or anything that even hints of platitudes about making beds or lying in them. Hey, as you'll read later, debt happens to most of us. It's what you do to make it work for you, rather than against you, that makes a difference.

DEBT: THE TRILLION-DOLLAR QUESTION

No one will deny that we're a nation of consumers hooked on credit. According to the Bank of Canada, our debt-to-disposable income ratio hit 130 percent in 2009, meaning we have more debt than income. Meanwhile, the Certified General Accountants Association of Canada reports that household debt reached an all-time high of $1.3 trillion in 2008 as more families reached for a credit card to finance day-to-day living expenses. Another report from The Vanier Institute of the Family states that in late 2008, the average total debt load per household was about $90,700. What's more, lines of credit and credit cards account for the lion's share of consumer debt, with 85 percent of Canadians admitting they have outstanding debt.

So if the *majority* of us are loading up credit cards, dipping into lines of credit, or buying now and paying later, is debt always such a bad thing? There must be an upside.

Absolutely. On the face of it, credit has a lot going for it. It's handy, for one. We can also rack up travel points or even get free groceries when we use certain cards. It lets us pay for something in today's prices instead of saving and possibly paying more later. And in a crisis? Having access to a line of credit is invaluable.

So what's the issue?

The problem with depending on credit is that for many of us, it's hard to know when to stop. The compulsive buyer, or shopaholic, fills closets with unworn clothing because there seems to be no limit to what money can be borrowed. It's also incredibly easy to find ourselves deeply in debt because that access to credit gives us the illusion we have more money than we actually do. We feel richer so we buy more.

This reliance on credit, which is becoming second nature to us, spurns us on to use credit to pay for items we never would have dreamed of purchasing that way 20 years ago. Throw in the fact that most of our fixed expenses continue to rise in cost, and it's easy to see how our collective spender-bender isn't the only thing working against us.

"The $1.3 trillion number is very disturbing," says Taylore Ashlie, director of communications for the Certified General Accountants Association of Canada. "Canadians need to know more about their financial situation. They need to know what debt means and what that debt will cost them."

Amen to that.

The question then becomes how do we determine debt's true impact on our bottom line? And is there a way to use debt wisely rather than allowing ourselves to lose control of it?

GOOD DEBT VS. BAD DEBT

The first thing to remember is that debt isn't inherently damaging. In fact, there are very good reasons why we don't, say, save our money for 25 years and then pay for a house in full. Here's why:

> Nadia wants to buy a $300,000 home outside of Toronto. She has $30,000 for her down payment and takes out a $270,000 mortgage at 6.35 percent interest and with an amortization period of 25 years. If she pays monthly over that 25-year span, she will pay $265,205.31 in interest. The total cost of the house? $565,205.31. It doesn't sound like much of a deal, does it?

But it could be worse. Her friend Angie also wants to buy a house for $300,000, but the mere idea of incurring debt makes her break out in hives. Angie's plan is to rent a $1,200 apartment and save $1,000 each month for 25 years so she can pay for the home outright the day she moves in. But over 300 months, that rent is a killer, costing Angie $360,000 in total. In effect, she has spent $660,000 on her home. She has also had to wait a quarter century for moving day.

DRIVE DOWN DEBT!

What are some warning signs that you have too much debt?

- You have no idea how much total debt you actually have.
- You lie to friends or family about your spending habits and debt load.
- You have little or no savings.
- You've maxed out at least one credit card.
- You make only minimum payments on your credit cards each month.
- You're still using your card to make purchases while trying to pay it off.
- You are occasionally late in making payments on bills, credit cards, or other expenses.
- You use cash advances from your credit cards to pay bills.
- You bounce cheques or overdraw your bank accounts.
- You receive calls from collection agents.
- You've been denied credit.

Want to know more? Hop online and find out where you stand. Go to Chatelaine.com and try our money quizzes. ■

Of course these scenarios have been overly simplified and don't take into account other variables, such as rental increases or any interest Angie might accumulate on her savings. Nadia's interest rate would surely change over the years. It also doesn't allow for the certainty that by the time Angie is ready to buy her $300,000 home, that same property would demand a much higher price. In other words, who knows what 300 grand would buy us 25 years from now?

So good debt is the debt you incur to buy an asset such as a house or other investment that you hope will appreciate in value over time. Good debt might also help you make money in the future, such as a student loan for your education. Bad debt, however, is debt you take on to buy stuff you want such as vacations or a fifth sweater you might not actually need. Furthermore, when you throw compound interest into the mix, that trip to Paris or fuzzy sweater costs much more than the price tag shows.

And therein lies the problem. While prime lending rates may be on the low end of the scale, credit cards charge much more interest, often in the 16.5 percent to 19.9 percent range on overdue balances. This number goes up even more when using department store cards. Credit cards also make it incredibly easy to pay the minimum balance, sometimes as little as $12 or two or three percent of the amount owed.

Paying such a minuscule amount each month, however, can lead to financial disaster, ensuring that you'll be paying for years instead of months. Yes, repaying the minimum amount sounds appealing because you can stretch the cost over a longer period, which makes large purchases more affordable. But interest changes everything because the debt's APR (or annual percentage rate) is not simply 12 times the basic monthly interest rate. The interest you build *earns interest too* and begins to snowball.

We all understand (in the abstract) that the longer it takes to pay something off, the more it ultimately costs. But how many of us have ever followed that through to really see the difference it makes in a single, simple purchase? Consider the following example:

Karen decides it's time to dump her old bed and buy a new one, so she heads to her favourite furniture store and looks around. Within minutes she finds the bed she wants. Even better, she discovers that if she signs up for the store's credit card, she'll get a 10 percent discount on her purchase. She goes for it and piles the $1,817 onto the card.

When the first statement arrives in the mail, Karen notes the 20 percent interest rate and dutifully pays the $50 minimum balance and congratulates herself for finding a way to sleep in a new bed in exchange for such a small price.

If Karen had taken the time to crunch a few numbers, however, she might not sleep so soundly each night. By paying the minimum balance and only a tiny portion of principal while allowing the interest to compound, it will take Karen over 11 years to be rid of her debt and will cost her a whopping $1,931 in interest. By then she might be on to her next bedroom set.

But let's back up for a moment and consider a different scenario. Let's say Karen decides to pay double that, or $100 per month. By paying only a little more each month, Karen's debt time horizon (industry lingo for an investment period) drops to 22 months and she pays only $322.64 in interest.

Now let's assume she decides she wants to be even more aggressive with her debt and throws a fixed payment of $150 at her card's balance each month. In 14 short months, Karen's bed is paid in full. And the interest? She pays $149.34.

Understanding how credit card interest compounds and taking that knowledge to heart by repaying your loan faster is only the first step to knocking down debt. Let's think about that interest rate for a moment. Karen's rate was quite high at 20 percent. If she had found a way to transfer her debt to a lower-rate card or line of credit, or asked for a rate reduction, she could have saved even more.

But keep reading, because there are even more fabulous yet simple ways to save money and make your credit cards work for, rather than against, you.

DRIVE DOWN DEBT!

Searching for a way to incur less credit card interest? While the most effective way is to pay off your purchases in full each month, that's not always an option if you're digging yourself out of debt today. Instead, switch over to a card that charges less interest than the one you're using now. And no, we're not saying you should jump on the next Platinum card offer that drops in your mailbox boasting a 3.9 percent interest rate for the next six months. (Not only will that rate eventually shoot sky-high, but many of these cards also charge an annual fee.)

While some high-rate cards offer bells and whistles, from free insurance for rental cars to airline points, the best deals are often found with the lower interest cards offered by the same banks. For example, a bank's Visa Classic Low Rate card might charge consumers 11.9 percent interest, while its Visa Classic charges 19.5 percent interest.

Which one would you ask to switch to?

Before you call up your credit card company and ask for a different card or shop around for an entirely new company, do your homework first. To find out which cards charge cheaper interest rates, check out the Financial Consumer Agency of Canada's credit card comparison list. Use your search engine and type in: "Financial Consumer Agency of Canada Credit Cards and You: Credit Card Comparison Tables" to land on the correct page. You can also go to their website directly at Fcac-acfc.gc.ca. ∎

KNOW YOUR FEES

"Good news! You've been pre-approved for a Super Gold Platinum Titanium Ultra Mega card with a low, low interest rate of 4.5 percent! Not only that, we consider you such an important client, we're happy to offer you eight free convenience cheques as well. And can we say again how incredibly special you are? Just send this card away today and find out for yourself!"

It's tempting to apply for a credit card that butters us up, makes us feel like we're part of an elite club, and promises us a card on the spot. And some of these cards can actually be a good deal if you know the rules and play by them. But before you sign anything, take a moment and ask yourself: do I understand the card's service fees and how they're structured? Most of us don't. Let's face it, credit card issuers may be required by law to tell us what service fees they charge, but that doesn't mean they make it easy for us to understand them.

But understanding the terms is crucial when shopping around for a new card or replacing the one you already have. Choose wisely and you can save yourself hundreds of dollars each year even before you calculate the interest you pay.

Here's a list of credit card transaction fees and what they actually mean to your bottom line:

ANNUAL FEES

Wondering why there's an extra $100 tacked on to your statement this month? A credit card's annual fee can be a nasty shock if you're expecting to pay $250 one month and discover you're on the hook for $350, but the upside to the fee is that it often means you're receiving a lower interest rate or more options such as airline points. (Points are really only useful, though, if you spend a lot, charge everything to your card and pay the bill in full each month.)

Still, if you usually carry a balance on your card, that low interest rate may save you money even if you're shelling out for the fee. For instance, if you carry a balance of $2,500 and pay a $50 annual fee (two percent of the total) on a card charging 9.99 percent interest, you're paying the equivalent of 11.99 percent interest. That sure beats a no-fee card charging 18.9 percent.

But why not go one step further? Particularly if you're a good customer who pays on time each month, call up your credit card issuer and ask to delete the fee. Many will. While $100 each year doesn't sound like much, after 10 years that's $1,000 in your pocket.

CASH ADVANCE FEES

You're down to a few dollars in your chequing account until Thursday, but you need some cash for incidentals now. Heading to the bank machine and withdrawing cash from your credit card sounds like a good idea, right?

We'll admit it's convenient, but before entering your PIN, be aware of what the service is going to cost you in cash advance fees. The fee might be in the form of a fixed amount (typically in the $1.25 to $5 range), a percentage of the amount taken (one to four percent), or a combination of both. It doesn't stop there, either. Interest is charged immediately so, unlike your credit card, there's no grace period to pay it back.

If you must use your credit card for a cash advance, pay off the balance as quickly as you can to avoid racking up interest charges. Don't wait for the statement to arrive.

CONVENIENCE CHEQUES

In the post-holiday letdown come January, your mailbox is probably full of them: convenience cheques. Also known as credit card cheques, they look like personal cheques you receive from the bank, but that's where the similarity ends. Credit card companies advertise them as convenient, easy ways to pay bills or gather some extra money, but look out. They're an expensive way to tackle a cash crunch since, like cash advances, they charge interest from the moment you use one.

OVER-THE-LIMIT FEES

Think that once you hit your card's credit limit, that new patio set will have to wait? Not always. Your credit card issuer decides whether it will allow you to make any over-the-limit purchases—and what fee you'll have to pay if you do. Check the credit card agreement you received when you first signed on for the card to find out how much you'll be dinged for being overdrawn (or call the company and ask for a new agreement if it has been a while since you got your card; the fee might have changed).

If you routinely have trouble with limiting your spending, ask for help from an unlikely place. Call the credit card company and ask them to put a stop to any transactions that exceed your credit limit so you can avoid paying over-the-limit fees. Some will offer the service, others won't, but it never hurts to ask.

Here's another tactic for those who occasionally want to buy more than their card allows: if you want to make a major purchase, and you think it might put you over your limit, call your credit card company first and ask for a credit limit increase. Just remember to lower it again later to avoid temptation.

INACTIVITY FEES

You've been really good this year, only using your two low interest credit cards and allowing the others to collect dust in a drawer. Unfortunately your idea of "good" and the credit issuer's idea of "good" are a tad different. If there's been a period of inactivity on a card—usually at least a year—you may get slapped with a fee because you haven't used the card!

Although it doesn't seem fair, it could be worse if you've been carrying a balance all of that time. Here's one scenario: let's say you bought a bottle of perfume for your mom five years ago on a store credit card and somehow an error sent the statements to the wrong address. It was a small purchase so you completely forget about it. That is, until you decide to take out a loan for a new car. The problem is that your credit report shows a long-standing unpaid balance and now your credit rating has taken a dive. But it gets worse. When the error is corrected, and you do receive the card's statement, not only has the interest compounded, costing you much more than the gift was worth, but you've been charged with an inactive credit balance fee to the tune of $125—or $25 each year.

As you can see, taking scissors to plastic doesn't automatically cancel them. If you no longer need your credit card, use it once or twice a year for small purchases until it expires. Before your card reaches its expiry date, call to inform your card issuer that you don't want a new one. Don't forget to get a confirmation in writing that the card is indeed cancelled and the balance is paid in full.

FOREIGN CURRENCY CONVERSION FEES

If you decide to use your credit card outside of Canada, you'll be charged a conversion fee as well as an exchange rate. Depending on whose card you use, that conversion fee varies from 1.8 to 2.5 percent of the transaction's amount. Since rates can vary from one credit card issuer to another, pull out your card agreements again and compare them.

DON'T FORGET GRACE PERIODS

Your credit card statement might display every purchase you made in a 30 or 31 day period (eek!), but you don't actually get that much time to pay off your balance without incurring interest. The time you do have is called your "grace period."

Until 2009, we had no mandatory grace period in Canada, but in 2009 the federal government mandated a minimum 21-day interest-free grace period on all new transactions when consumers paid their balance in full by the due date. This new regulation also requires card issuers to clearly display information about grace periods and interest rates in a summary box on bills. So as soon as you receive your statement in the mail, write down the due date.

WHICH CREDIT CARD SHOULD I CHOOSE?

Use this worksheet to compare interest rates and service fees. Don't forget to consider which features will mean the most to you and which ones you can do without. For example, if you rarely travel, you might want to skip the card with competitive foreign currency conversion rates, or else risk paying for something you don't use.

Worksheet No. 4

	Card A	**Card B**	**Card C**
Credit card issuer			
Card name			
Type of card (Basic, Gold, etc.)			
Annual interest rate			
Promotional rate			
Length of time that rates apply			
Cash advance interest rate			
Balance transfer interest rate			
Annual fee			
First card			
Extra cards			
Duration of grace period			
Rewards program			
Time it takes to accumulate enough reward points to reach your goal			
Insurance benefits offered			
Cash advance fee in Canada			
Cash advance fee outside Canada			
Over-the-limit fee			
Foreign currency conversion fee			
Inactivity fee			
Other			

DO YOU DEBIT?

Credit cards aren't the only plastic swiped in stores today. Debit cards, used to access money in bank accounts, are incredibly popular in Canada. In fact, Canada is one of the largest debit card markets in the world, second only to Sweden. In 2007, we were responsible for nearly three and a half billion _Interac_ "direct transactions," primarily as in-store purchases.

So why do our bank cards reign supreme at the till? Maybe because they offer some definite advantages over credit cards: they don't charge interest—it's your money after all—and they're more convenient than walking around with $250 in your purse. Even more importantly, you're paying with money you already have so they make it harder to overextend yourself and go into debt. Store owners like them too, and hope you'll use your debit cards over credit cards because of their more affordable merchant fees.

Still, there's also a dark side to debit. Taking a swipe at debit cards is as simple as pointing out the 50 cent fee charged each time you make a purchase (unless your bank covers a set number of those each month). And watch out for bank overdraft fees if you dip into the red zone. They can be a killer.

Then there's also the fact that for many of us, it's easier psychologically to rack up purchases with a debit card in hand. Studies into credit versus cash payments seem to bear this out, going so far as to say that we're likelier to spend more money by eschewing cash. Want proof? Try this: walk up to the till with a $75 sweater and pay for it in cash. You'll probably feel the weight of the transaction more keenly than simply pushing some plastic across the counter. By dissociating ourselves from the actual cost of the purchase, it becomes a case of see no money, pay no money.

GET OUT OF DEBT—FASTER!

It all begins with the brain. What's your personality? Are you a risk taker or someone who takes a more cautious approach? When it comes to anything financial, you've got to do what works for you, not what the popular TV financial guru advises or what your best friend suggests. If you can't stand running a low bank balance at the end of each month because you've been aggressively going after your debt, it won't take long before you panic and backtrack, or quit altogether. Or maybe you're all fired up and need a fast-and-furious approach to keep motivated.

Whatever method you choose, be sure to ask yourself two questions before digging in and paying out:

1. Why did I get into debt in the first place?

2. What do I need to do so it doesn't happen again?

Equate your payback plan to a diet. Dieters who ask these questions before heading out on the walking trail for the first time or whipping up a low-cal breakfast are much more likely to keep the pounds off for good. They know their weaknesses and they come up with ways to defeat them. So, for example, if you had a comfortable debt load until you lost your job, maybe you need to build a larger cash emergency fund. If, however, you can't pass a sale without whipping out the plastic, leave the cards at home and break the habit.

KNOW WHAT YOU OWE

Melissa had no idea her debt situation was so dire because she never bothered to figure out what she owed. And because she kept herself in the dark, those loans kept creeping up, up, and up. But understanding your debt load is a crucial step to going debt free. Take a deep breath, gather your bills and bank statements, and use this worksheet to determine where your money needs to go.

HOW MUCH DO I OWE?

Worksheet No. 5

What I owe	$ total amount owed	$ owed per month (total divided by 12)	Interest rate (if relevant)	Whom do I owe money to?	Action I'm taking
Taxes					
Credit cards					
Personal loan					
Other personal loan					
Car payments					
Alimony					
Child support					
Student loan					
Other debt					
Total excluding housing					
Back rent or mortgage					
Total with housing					

LOWER YOUR INTEREST

One of the easiest ways to shake off debt's handcuffs is to transfer the amount you owe to the lowest-interest line of credit or loan you qualify for. For example, if you were to pay off a balance of $15,000 at 18 percent interest, with monthly payments of $600, it will take 32 months to pay it off and will cost you $3,941 in interest. Now say you transfer that balance to a line of credit at seven percent. You'll be debt free in 28 months, making the same monthly payment—and you'll only pay $1,261 in interest, a savings of $2,680.

Lowering the interest on your high-cost plastic, however, can be as simple as calling your card-issuing company. If you have a good history of paying at least the minimum balance on your cards, chances are very good that your rate will be lowered on the spot. Call and politely say that you've been a loyal customer for years, but the competition has offered you a better rate. Then ask if the company can beat it. A new rate of 10 to 12 percent is reasonable, but see how low they'll go.

CONSOLIDATE YOUR DEBT

If you have a solid credit rating and some form of collateral, you could probably qualify for a consolidated loan—a bank loan you use to pay off various debts, leaving you with one debt, generally at a better interest rate and with only one monthly payment to keep track of.

There is a danger to consolidated loans, however. Some estimates indicate that up to 80 percent of people who take out consolidated loans go on to run up further debts and find themselves in even more perilous financial straits. That doesn't have to be your story! Remember: a consolidated loan only amalgamates your debts; you haven't wiped them out. So figure out why you're in debt, hide your credit cards, and focus on paying off the loan first.

REFINANCE YOUR HOUSE

Sometimes getting a handle on your payments is as simple as refinancing your mortgage. If you decide to go to your bank halfway through a five-year term, for instance, increase the amount you owe (that extra money borrowed goes to paying off your debts)—but keep your interest at the same rate. As long as the debt isn't too outrageous, you'll probably only pay a few extra dollars each week instead of hundreds. Take the money you save and use it to build an emergency fund or max out RRSPs.

GET A LOAN (REALLY!)

Can you ask family or friends for a gift or an interest-free or low-interest loan to help get you out of debt? Tell them why you need the money, draw up a contract and payment schedule, and stick to it. Or go to the bank and ask for a lower interest loan—not a line of credit. Why? A line of credit, unless it's a fixed payment line of credit, is too easy to dip in to and can eventually make the situation worse. Knowing that you have to pay a set amount each month for a finite amount of time works.

DIP INTO YOUR RRSPs AND OTHER LOANS

Does the thought make you want to reach for a stiff drink? Guess what: RRSPs aren't always the sacred cow some financial planners make them out to be, especially if you have a lot of unused contribution room. If you're earning eight percent interest on your RRSP asset and paying 18 percent interest on your credit card debt, saving money is more illusion than reality. Crunch the numbers and see if RRSPs make sense for you right now.

Let's be honest here. Although it would be nice to continually save for retirement for 30 years, there are stages in our lives that are downright expensive (think the daycare-mortgage double whammy in our thirties) and continuous saving can seem more like a pipe dream. Don't beat yourself up about it.

Once you've paid off your debt, talk to your financial advisor about balancing your RRSP withdrawal with a low-interest RRSP loan (usually easy to qualify for) that can be used to reinvest, lower taxes, and get you back on track.

Remember that if you cash in your RRSPs, that money is included in your taxable income and you will have to pay income tax on it. If it also means you're also going to be pushed into a higher tax bracket, talk to a financial advisor before you cash in your RRSPs to see if she has any other recommendations for debt reduction.

If you decide to cash in other investments to cancel out a debt, again, talk to a financial expert first and pinpoint investments that have the fewest early withdrawal penalties and back-end load fees.

ROLL IT OVER

Now that you've reduced your interest, it's payback time. Eliminate debt fast and create momentum. Some call it "restructuring debts for accelerated payoff," others call it the "rollover" technique. Whatever moniker you use, here's how it works:

1. Make a list of all of your debts.

2. Sort your debts from highest interest rate to lowest.

3. Figure out how much money you put toward paying down your debts each month.

4. Continue to pay the same monthly amount, but restructure your spending so that you only pay minimum payments on all except the highest rate debt.

5. Once the debt with the killer rate is paid off, move down your list and apply your savings to the next highest rate debt.

6. And so on and so on . . .

Not only does the rollover technique allow you to pay off debts faster (there are plenty of accelerated debt payoff calculators online that will show you how much money you'll save and how quickly the debt is wiped clean. A good one can be found at Smartaboutmoney.org), it's also a good way to give yourself an emotional boost as each debt gets wiped off the list.

Again, consider your personality before deciding which debt to tackle first. While many financial experts advise that we pay off the loan, no matter how large or small, with the heftiest interest rate first, some say it's more satisfying to pick off debts with a smaller balance before tackling the big one. Either way, once the momentum starts and you're able to see the light at the end of the tunnel, you'll be less inclined to go back to your spendthrift ways.

START SMALL

Another option to get out of the minimum payment trap is by setting up automatic money transfers through online banking. Transferring an extra $25 a week from your bank account to pay off a credit card or student loan—an amount few of us would even miss—adds up to an extra $1,300 a year. Then, as your debt decreases, increase your weekly transfer amount. In just a few short years you will have zapped though your loans and debts.

GET WITH THE (STUDENT LOAN) PLAN

Students who have graduated and are having a difficult time paying off their loan should look into the new federal student loan Repayment Assistance Plan. The plan makes it easier for student loan borrowers to manage their debt by paying back what they can reasonably afford. According to the federal government's website, borrowers on the plan should not have to take longer than 15 years to pay off their debt (or 10 years for those with permanent disabilities); affordable student loan payments should be based on the size and income of borrowers' families; and borrowers' payments shouldn't exceed 20 percent of their family income. Check out Canlearn.ca and your provincial or territorial student-assistance centre for more information.

KEEP AT IT

It's funny what can happen to us when a debt is finally wiped clean. There's that delicious moment of freedom when the last dollar is paid. But, let's be honest, life has a habit of throwing us curveballs and erasing our memories. So if that zero balance on your credit card feels like an open invitation for a celebratory shopping spree, take a moment and think before hitting the racks. Keeping the shrieks of debt down to a dull roar is a lifelong goal. Keep at it.

FICO SAVINGS

What's your credit score? Unsure? It's time to fire up your computer and check the credit bureaus' websites or reach for the phone and find out. Your credit rating, or score—the somewhat complicated statistical method of determining the likelihood that you'll pay back a loan—is not just a number, but worth thousands of dollars in savings because creditors use it to decide how much risk you pose when they lend you money. If you're deemed a higher risk, they'll charge you more in interest and other fees to offset that risk. Low-risk borrowers, however, enjoy better rates because the lender is pretty sure they're going to pay up and on time.

With a great score, you'll be offered—and you'll be able to negotiate—better deals from mortgages to credit card rates. Those zero-percent financing bargains? They generally go to people with spotless credit reports and high FICO scores. (FICO stands for Fair Isaac Corporation, the company that created the system used to calculate credit scores.)

TAKE A NUMBER

If you want to know your credit score in Canada, you'll want to contact the two main credit-reporting agencies: TransUnion and Equifax. They analyze your financial history and create scores to try and predict your behaviour in 10 years' time based on how similar you are to people who repay loans promptly. Scores are measured from 300 to 900; you want to have a score of at least 650 when applying for any kind of loan. One below is considered "poor" or "very poor" and will make it hard to get credit. Your score is considered "great" if it hits 750 or above. According to Equifax, the average Canadian checks in at 751; TransUnion reports that 47 percent of Canadians rank in the "great" range. Twelve percent of Canadians have a score of less than 600.

FIND OUT WHERE YOU STAND

If you're about to take out a loan and don't want any surprises, or simply want to build a complete picture of your finances, check with both TransUnion (Transunion.ca) and Equifax (Equifax.ca). Both credit bureaus use different formulas and because you never know which one your lender will contact, it's good to know how you rank with both and if all of the information they have on you is accurate. For about $30 each, they'll email you a detailed report that includes your score, a credit history that details your bill payments for the past six years, and an explanation of how you rank compared to the general population. Both companies provide tips to boost your score. You can also write away to either company for a free basic credit-history report—which doesn't include your score—once a year.

MAKE CHANGES

Now that you have your score, do you like what you see? If you think there's room for improvement, know that the one habit that will help you the most is always making at least your minimum payments on time. Agencies can't see if you're throwing $36 at your debt or $160 each month, but they can see if you hit the minimum, paid late, or missed payments entirely. So even if your bill is for $10 or $15, pay up or risk a spotty credit rating. On the bright side, if you missed payments or even had a loan go to a collections agency more than six years ago, that black mark is scrubbed clean today.

DON'T BELIEVE THE HYPE

There's a common myth circulating that the more credit you qualify for, the better. Of course if you have no credit history at all, you're considered a higher risk borrower because lenders see you as the great unknown. But few of us have that problem since we've been paying bills for years.

So what happens if you've mistakenly picked up six, seven, or eight cards thinking it would help your cause? A potential creditor would probably total your maximum limits, say $40,000, and decide you could get into $40,000 of debt plus whatever else you borrow. So use only one or two cards and call the card company to ask for a lower maximum for the rest, or cancel cards in reverse chronological order so you're keeping the cards you've had longest. They're your ticket to keeping your long credit history in the system. And continue paying down your debt. Keeping your balance to less than 35 percent of your total limit improves your score. Less debt and a smaller credit limit is your one-two punch.

REAP THE REWARDS

Play the numbers game and it won't be long before you see an improvement. The good news is that most people can raise their scores in just a few months. So check your scores, see what you owe, and pay it off as fast as you can. Pretty soon you'll be in the zero-percent financing club too.

PAYDAY LOANS NEVER PAY

"Need cash? Why wait until payday? $100 or more. Fast!"

You've probably seen the ads referring to payday loans, cash advance loans, cheque advance loans, post-dated cheque loans, or deferral deposit loans. Whatever you call them, these small-amount, short-term, high-interest loans offered by finance companies come at a very high price.

Here's how they typically work:

Talia is out of cash and her credit cards are maxed out so she can't turn to them for a cash advance. Instead, she walks into a payday loan issuer's storefront office. She writes them a cheque for the amount she wants to borrow until payday—$200—plus the company's fee of 25 percent of the cheque's face value ($50, in this case). The lender gives her the $200 and agrees to hold the cheque until the loan is due before cashing it in. The lender also gives her the option of automatically depositing the amount into her chequing account, minus the fee.

It's easy to see why the payday loan volume in Canada is estimated at $2 billion a year, with loan offices springing up all over the country.

Historically, payday loans have been pricey and problematic for those using them regularly. Most provinces and territories now have stricter rules and regulations to ensure stronger consumer protection. But until recently Canadians could get themselves in serious trouble by taking out new loans before the old ones were paid.

Instead of a payday loan, consider a small loan from a credit union or consumer-friendly financial institution, shop for credit with a low interest rate, contact your creditors if you're having trouble making payments and ask for more time to pay up or find out if your bank will offer you overdraft protection. ■

THE UNTHINKABLE: BANKRUPTCY

Jennifer and her husband Steve live in Moncton and struggle to make ends meet each month even though Steve sometimes works two jobs while Jennifer takes care of their three small children at home. They're trying to do the right thing, paying off at least part of the bills, getting credit counselling, and even going through a consumer proposal process. But eventually, as bills pile up again, the couple finds themselves deciding between paying them and paying for food for the kids.

And now that creditors are calling them at home demanding payment they can't afford, the stress is unbearable.

"We've tried so hard, but I feel we don't have a choice at this point. Bankruptcy might be our only option," Jennifer says.

No one *wants* to declare bankruptcy. The process is long, arduous, and emotionally draining. And it isn't a get out of jail free card, since bankruptcies are recorded at credit bureaus for up to six years and every loan grantor will be able to see them. You may also be forced to give up some of your assets and hand over a portion of your paycheque to pay off your creditors.

But sometimes bankruptcy is the last option for people who have experienced unemployment, sickness, divorce, or have racked up debt they will never afford to pay off. If this sounds like your situation, you might want to know that you're not the only one in this predicament. About 100,000 Canadians each year file for bankruptcy, and that number is on the rise.

While bankruptcy will stop creditors from harassing you and prevent them from garnishing your wages, the true purpose of bankruptcy is to allow a debtor to get a fresh financial start and help creditors collect at least a portion of their money.

So how do you know if you're a candidate for bankruptcy? First of all, you need to be deemed insolvent. That means:

1. You owe at least $1,000.

2. You're not able to meet your debts when payment is due.

Put it this way: if you've tried all the other alternatives—contacting creditors and asking for a payment plan, contacting a qualified credit counsellor, or filing a consumer proposal (a trustee asks for a reduction of what you owe and you make payments that reflect the new plan)—but your minimum monthly bills are still more than you can pay, bankruptcy is probably your last option.

Here are steps you'll take if you decide to declare bankruptcy:

1. You'll meet with a trustee in bankruptcy. This is the person licensed to administer the bankruptcy process. Find a trustee in your area by searching the Yellow Pages or searching the Web (type in "bankruptcy trustee" + your province or city). Remember, the trustee actually works on behalf of your creditors, not you.

2. The trustee files for bankruptcy after meeting with you and going over your financial situation. Once the trustee files, you are declared bankrupt and creditors can no longer take any legal action against you. You are also no longer required to make payments.

3. Your creditors are notified. Sometimes a meeting of creditors is called for, but unless your outstanding debt is very large that usually doesn't happen.

4. Your assets are turned over to the trustee so they can be dispersed amongst your creditors. Some assets are exempt by federal and provincial laws. Your trustee can advise you of what you can keep and what you'll lose. You'll also be required to make monthly payments to the trustee—if possible—and that money will be dispersed too.

5. You'll attend two financial counselling sessions at the trustee's office to learn financial management. Some sessions are private and others are held with other people in a class setting.

6. If you've done everything the trustee asks of you, he or she will prepare a report and recommend that you be discharged from your debts. Most, but not all, bankruptcies are eligible for discharge after the minimum period of nine months. You'll be sent a copy of the discharge for your own files.

As you can see, the process is pretty straightforward for most people who declare bankruptcy in Canada, but there are a couple more issues you'll want to be aware of.

Note that if you file for bankruptcy, your debts are your debts, and you are the only one responsible for them. Your husband, partner, or common-law spouse is not. The only exception is if your spouse has co-signed or guaranteed your debt at the time you both took out the loan. Also, there are a few debts that bankruptcy does not eliminate: child support, alimony, back taxes, and debts due to fraud or theft. (So if your ex pleads bankruptcy as the reason he can't pay up, you can respond with, "And this is my problem because . . .?")

So let's say you've done it. Your debts are now discharged and bankruptcy is burning a hole in your credit report. You're probably feeling embarrassed. But don't wallow for more than a few moments, because guess what? If you think about it, bankruptcy is a wake-up call and an opportunity to get your financial house back in order. Your slate is clean and now you can make amends and show everybody how you've turned your life around.

Jennifer and Steve did. After going through financial counselling together and meeting with the trustee, they discovered they were spending much more money on incidentals than they thought. Jennifer started purchasing perfectly good clothes for her kids from the consignment shops instead of buying new. Her husband asked for a raise and got it. Jennifer is even selling her services as a kid's bedroom decorator after her friends pushed her to turn her passion into a business. Making the decision to file for bankruptcy was a tough one, Jennifer admits, but it did help them to re-evaluate their finances.

GET EDUCATED

Looking for more bankruptcy information? Here are a few trustworthy websites to check out:

- Bankruptcy-canada.ca
- Nomoredebts.org
- Creditcounsellingcanada.ca (This site helps find a reputable credit counsellor in your area.) ∎

WATCH MONEY GROW

Remember compound interest? Earlier in this chapter we discussed how compound interest can turn a little bit of debt into a huge pile of worry, but what if you found out the same principle can work in your favour? It can. Now that you know how to spend smart and slash debt without losing any more sleep, keep reading to find out how to make the money you save grow.

Chapter 4

INVEST IN YOURSELF

....

*Trista, a 33-year-old bookstore employee and artist in Ottawa,
can't believe it when she discovers her grandmother has
bequeathed her $200,000. Nobody had any idea the elderly
woman was sitting on so much money! But when Trista picks
up her cheque a few weeks later, she's suddenly struck with the
realization that she is clueless about what do with it. The only
investment she holds is an apartment full of paperbacks. And her
portfolio? It's crammed with her artwork—not stocks or bonds.*

*Trista knows she needs to find financial help fast so she turns
to her money-savvy uncle. He recommends a certified financial
planner at a well-known brokerage firm. When Trista sits
down with her planner and explains that she can't stomach
losses, he sells her what seems like a safe bet: a mutual fund.
Unfortunately, even after he conducts a risk analysis, that
fund isn't as low-risk as Trista wants. It holds mostly aggressive
growth stocks that could shoot up in value—or tank. What's
more, when she receives her first statement, there is a
thousand dollars missing.*

"Oh, that?" says her now much-less-popular planner. "I'm paid a two percent commission out of your investment. Didn't I mention that?"

It takes two more attempts to find unbiased help before Trista finally gets what she needs: a fee-for-service advisor who helps her build a financial plan, offers some extra tips, then agrees to step back until she has questions later on. The advisor even understands Trista's point when she explains why, despite being young and therefore in a better position to take on more risk, she wants to go with a more conservative approach for her portfolio—45 percent bonds and GICs.

"I'm an artist and make $12 an hour working at the bookstore. I can't see my financial picture changing any time soon, either, so my inheritance is my nest egg. I can't lose this money. Once I explained my point to her, my advisor got it," Trista says.

D O YOU "GET" INVESTING? ALL RIGHT, LET'S REPHRASE that. Do you feel confident, knowledgeable, and excited when you think about investing your money so you can buy a cottage, retire early, or travel the globe some day? Do you know what your RRSPs are earning? Do you know how to read a prospectus? Can you honestly raise your hand and say, "Yes, when it comes to investing, I have it all figured out!"?

Maybe you can, but according to numerous surveys, you're in the minority. In fact, according to the oft-quoted Women Cents Study, developed by the National Center for Women and Retirement Research in the U.S., three-quarters of the women surveyed said their lack of knowledge about how to select financial instruments was their biggest stumbling block to becoming more active investors. More than half postponed financial decisions for fear of making a mistake, and 58 percent worried after making a big investment decision.

And who can blame so many of us for feeling this way? People put off what they don't understand, and as one of the first generations of women to be expected to carry our own financial weight after years of social and cultural baggage, it's no easy thing to suddenly throw it all aside and say, "Today, I'm going to find out how to invest in a REIT." Not only do you have to know what a real-estate investment trust is, but, between work, dishes, shuttling kids around to play dates or dance lessons, groceries, and maybe a little hanky-panky after dark with your equally exhausted (yet hopeful) spouse, who has time to do investment homework?

You do.

Because here's a secret: investing doesn't have to be brain draining or time consuming. And if you take 30 minutes to read this chapter, you'll pick up fabulous tips about hiring a professional planner to keep you on track, learn some tried and true investment basics—all you need to know to watch your money grow—how to decide the amount of risk you'll want to take on, and other concepts to increase your knowledge and give your confidence a boost.

Will you ever make money blunders? Yes, you will. We all do. But it is a big mistake to allow the fear of failure to keep you from managing your money so that you can live your dreams today or when you're a fearless, 63-year-old, globe-trotting, sangria-mixing matriarch. Remember that money fear is just fear. It's not proof that the financial risk you're going to take is a bad idea.

So keep reading. Investing some time today will pay off in dividends later. Literally.

SHOULD YOU HIRE HELP?

To hire a financial planner or not to hire a financial planner. It's a choice all of us have to make when it comes time to manage our money. Although sometimes it's an obvious one—you've come into a pile of cash and have no idea what to do with it—for the rest of us who have smaller funds to work with, the choice isn't always so clear-cut. We know a bit about mutual funds. We have an inkling about why RRSPs are a good idea. And GICs are supposed to be stress-free, right?

Let's take a look at the pros and cons of hiring a professional versus doing your own investing.

The upside to hiring a financial planner or advisor:

- **They have the time.** You might be burning the candle at both ends, and sometimes in the middle too, but your financial planner's job is to make time for your money.

- **They have the knowledge.** Most planners have the necessary education to be able to write financial plans, provide advice and are licensed to sell stocks, bonds and mutual funds. A good one you like and trust will help educate you as well so you know where your money is going and why.

- **They don't get emotional.** Buy low and sell high, right? That's a lot easier to do when it's not your own money on the line. A financial advisor will remind you that even if the economy is on its way down, you're investing for the long term so hang tight. This is only a blip along the way to retirement.

- **They're all about goal setting.** Do you know how much you actually need for retirement? Do you know how long you have to save for that car you're coveting? How much do you need to sock away each month? A planner calculates all of these numbers for you and gets you started.

- **You don't feel alone.** For some people, managing money solo can seem too intimidating or boring. By buddying up with an advisor you've got company— and someone to advise you if you suddenly have to cash in an investment.

The downside to hiring:

- **They can cost you—a lot.** Remember that two percent fee Trista paid? Annual fees, commissions, and back-end loads take a serious chunk out of your earnings, even if the interest rate you reap is high. What's more, an advisor typically takes between .25 percent and one percent of your assets annually, which, although it sounds small, can still add up over time. Look for planners and advisors who invest in pools with no or low front loads and back loads in order to keep your costs down.

- **You get the same returns.** If you know a few rules about balancing a portfolio, diversifying, and finding investments that tend to do well over time, chances are your investments will experience the same performance.

- **You might make more money if you're more aggressive with your investment plan.** Are you hooked on risk? A lot of advisors won't touch you since they're all about long-term planning and sticking to the rules. If you choose to be your own investment advisor, however, you get to do what *you* want with your money without answering to anybody.

- **Some advisors are not as ethical as their profession dictates.** Always do your research and get referrals before hiring a professional.

- **Investing is fun.** That is, if you educate yourself, read everything you can get your hands on, ask a lot of questions, and know how to play the game. Watching your money grow because you've made some smart financial moves is incredibly satisfying.

Also, remember that some financial planners only work with high net-worth individuals—people with more than $100,000 in liquid assets to manage. So even if you've found a fantastic advisor, there's a chance she won't work with you.

Find someone close to your age, advises Kathy McMillan, a certified financial planner with Richardson Partners Financial Limited in Calgary.

"If you're a young gal just starting out, you should be looking for a young planner just starting out too," she says.

For instance, a 36-year-old investor will more likely click with a thirtysomething advisor who understands her mortgage-kids-work-no-sleep world. An older advisor understands the concerns leading up to retirement. Because most veteran planners tend to take on only well-heeled clientele, hiring a slightly less experienced professional even has benefits: they're looking for clients and have more time for you.

HOW DO I FIND ONE?

So, let's say you would still prefer to pay for outside help. Whose door are you going to go knocking on when it comes time to hire? Start by asking around.

"Referrals are just great," says McMillan, who suggests asking money-savvy friends who they use. She's right. If a friend likes her financial advisor and sings his praises, that usually says something about his skill. Or try checking out Fpsccanada.org, the Financial Planners Standards Council's database of planners across Canada, or Advocis, Canada's largest association of financial advisors. But even if your best friend gives you the name of her financial planner, don't treat it as gospel. As Trista's story illustrates, a good word isn't always a reliable way to determine a planner's skill or ethics.

So once you have a planner on the phone, ask questions before agreeing to meet to make sure a longer meeting would be worth your time. Is the planner licensed? What's her investment philosophy? Does she work mainly with younger people—"money accumulators" in biz speak—or retirees?

Shop around until you're comfortable with the answers. McMillan recommends interviewing at least three people: one from the bank, one from an insurance company, and an independent. You might want to try a brokerage too. Then go with your gut.

"Do your homework," she says. "This is a long, intimate relationship."

ASK THESE QUESTIONS
BEFORE HIRING ANYONE:

1. **How are you paid? What percentage comes from the fees that I pay versus commissions from the products you sell?**

   Best answer: 100 percent of the planners' income comes from fees paid by clients. If a financial professional is paid by commission, get the fees in writing so there are no surprises.

   Walk away: All of the income relies on commission provided by the products the advisor is selling and you were not warned.

2. **If you're a fee-only advisor, do you charge an hourly fee for advice, or do I pay for ongoing money management?**

   Best answer: That depends on what you want. Paying by the hour gets you objective, specific financial advice and recommendations. A planner paid by the hour, or who charges a flat fee for certain things, might draft a financial plan for you after listening to you talk about what you want your money to do for you. A money manager is more hands-on and you pay her as she goes. (By the way, you can hire a money manager inexpensively through a mutual fund.)

   Walk away: Some advisors tell you they're fee-only and they're not, or they actually own two businesses: one fee-only, and another than sells products. So if you're suddenly asked to pay more than you initially agreed upon—and that was not part of the initial plan—start looking elsewhere for a new advisor.

3. **What is your hourly fee?**

   Best answer: Fees are all over the map, from $50 to several hundreds of dollars an hour. Typically though, most charge between $100 and $150 per hour.

Walk away: You pay the hourly fee then end up shelling out even more in hidden commissions later. Instead, find an advisor who is upfront about what they offer. Maybe that *does* turn out to be a fee-based model, which charges a client a fee for writing a financial plan, but investments warrant a commission withdrawn on a monthly or quarterly basis. An ethical advisor will give you a compensation discloser, a letter of engagement that outlines what both parties should expect, as well as a one-page document that divulges the advisor's clearly articulated investment philosophy. Ideally you want all of this in writing and with client sign-off.

4. **What experience do you have and what are your certifications?**

   Best answer: An advisor should have at least five years in the industry and some kind of certification such as a CFP or CLU behind her name. (But there are some newer financial planners who are still very good and looking for clients.) They should also be updating skills and knowledge through professional development.

   Typical designations include: CFP (Certified Financial Planner); CLU (Chartered Life Underwriter); ChFC (Chartered Financial Consultant—specialized in retirement planning); CIM (Canadian Investment Management); and RFP (Registered Financial Planner). To find out what they all mean, visit the Financial Advisors Association of Canada website at Advocis.ca.

   Walk away: Financial planners are sometimes tempted to say they have more industry experience than they actually do—they're only 32 years old but say they have 15 years of experience, for example. They want you to feel comfortable letting them make big decisions about your money. While small fibs about age probably don't amount to much, they might lead you to question other things that the advisor tells you.

5. **Can you provide references of people who have similar needs to mine?**

Best answer: Your planner should be able to say, "Of course. Here are three telephone numbers of clients who have agreed to act as references. Feel free to call them." Once you have the references on the phone, ask what the advisor's strengths and weaknesses are, and if they would hire her again, now knowing what they know.

Walk away: The advisor doesn't have references or tries to get you to come to a "free" session to meet in person instead. "My clients' names are confidential, but if you come to see me in person, I'm sure you'll get a sense of how I work," they might say. Hold the phone. Sometimes (not always, but sometimes) these free sessions are used simply to sell products.

BE YOUR OWN INVESTMENT ADVISOR

Investing in the stock market without an advisor at your side might seem risky, but just remember that the experts don't know what's going to happen in the markets tomorrow either. Remember back to the fall of 2008 when global markets went into convulsions after the U.S. investment bank Lehman Brothers shuttered its doors in New York? Who predicted *that*?

"I've come to the conclusion that nobody has any idea what is going to happen, what is happening, and when whatever is happing is going to end," says Rhonda Sherwood, a certified financial planner and financial management advisor with ScotiaMcLeod in Vancouver. "The markets aren't efficient. They're driven by facts and emotion."

Now, as we've discussed, a good financial advisor has a lot going for her. But even planners admit they don't have a crystal ball. (If they did, how many of them do you think would still be schlepping other people's money around?) So there's absolutely nothing wrong with trying to buy stocks or mutual funds yourself. You just have to do your homework first. Here's how:

1. **Learn the fundamentals.** Read this book and other personal finance material, and take a crash course in money basics by visiting Chatelaine.com or Canadianbusiness.com, and while you're at it, check out Investored.ca.

2. **Make a plan.** If you want to buy a house in five years, figure out how much money you'll need to set aside each month to build that down payment and have enough left over for legal fees and extras. Short-term investments (less than five years) are better suited to vehicles like guaranteed investment certificates (GICs) or tax-free savings accounts (TFSAs). But if you're in it for the long haul, go with stock-based investments.

3. **Consider a plan for the time-challenged.** Newbie investors do well with building a portfolio containing index funds—a type of mutual fund—and exchange-traded funds (ETFs).

4. **Get into stocks.** Yearning to be more hands-on? You can try the stock market, but it will cost you—and we're talking time, not money. Visit Canadianbusiness.com to read up on where you're putting your money. Articles will give you information about what companies are doing behind the scenes and why it might have an impact on your investments. You can also find stock quotes and set up a personalized database of funds to watch

5. **Mull over mutual funds.** Not ready for stocks, but want to see more action than an index provides? Go for mutual funds, although they might not perform as well as stocks.

Spoiler alert: we'll be discussing the couch potato portfolio, stocks, and mutual funds a little later.

KNOW THE TERMS

Even if you do decide to work with a financial planner, it's still an incredibly smart move to educate yourself about all things monetary. Why? Well, you're going to want to understand where your money is being invested and the reasons for that decision. Handing over your hard-earned assets to a stranger without appreciating the repercussions of his or her choices is a lot like driving your car to the mechanic, paying $500 to fix a rattle, and having no idea if you've just been fleeced. Knowing what an axel, spark plug, or crankshaft actually does allows you to talk shop, and helps make your mechanic feel that much more accountable.

What's more, if you decide to take the DIY approach, learning financial speak is also the first step to making your own choices that not only save you money in fees and commissions, but also give you a real sense of satisfaction and power. You're in the driver's seat with a clear view down the road.

Here is a short glossary of money terms you'll want to bone up on before we start discussing investment strategies:

ANNUITY: Essentially, a series of (usually monthly) payments doled out to a person from a lump sum investment. Retirees most often use annuities as a form of their retirement income.

ARBITRAGE: Purchasing an asset at one price and simultaneously selling it at a higher price on a different market in order to make a profit. Recommended for experienced investors only.

BEAR MARKET: A market condition, which tends to be accompanied by widespread pessimism, in which the prices of securities are falling or are expected to fall. An investor can be said to have bearish characteristics. See related term: bull market.

BLUE CHIP: The stock of companies such as Coca-Cola, IBM, or General Electric that have proven long-term track records. The term comes from poker where blue chips have the highest value.

BOND: Essentially an IOU, a bond is a debt instrument issued by a government or corporation in order to raise money. Basically, it obligates the issuer (the government or company) to pay the bondholder (you) the original amount of the loan plus interest on a specified maturity date.

BROKER: An intermediary who acts as a link between investors who wish to purchase a particular investment and those who wish to sell it. Generally, the broker charges a fee or commission related to the amount of money involved in the transaction.

BULL MARKET: A market condition in which the prices of securities are rising or are expected to rise. It tends to be associated with increasing investor confidence. See related term: bear market.

CANADA PENSION PLAN (CPP): A government pension that provides contributors and their families with disability, survivor, death, and children's benefits.

CANADA SAVINGS BOND (CSB): A type of bond issued each year by the federal government that offers a competitive interest rate and is redeemable at any time for its full face value. In recent years, CSBs have suffered a slip in popularity as investors increasingly choose to place their money elsewhere, such as an online high-interest savings account with ING DIRECT.

CAPITAL GAIN: A realized profit that results from the appreciation of a capital asset, such as stocks, bonds, or real estate, over its purchase price.

CERTIFICATE: A physical document that provides evidence of ownership of a security such as a stock or bond.

COMMODITIES: The raw materials of commerce such as gold, wheat, coffee, and pork bellies. Traders in commodities buy and sell contracts (also called futures) for such materials.

COMPOUND INTEREST: Interest that is calculated not only on the principal but also on accumulated interest.

DIVERSIFICATION: The practice of putting money into a number of different investments in order to reduce risk. The hope is that the positive performance of some investments will offset the negative performance of others.

DIVIDENDS: Payments made by a corporation to its shareholders.

DOW JONES INDUSTRIAL AVERAGE (DJIA): Frequently referred to as the Dow, this is the oldest and most widely followed stock index in the world. It tracks the performance of 30 blue chip stocks traded on the New York Stock Exchange (NYSE). It is generally regarded as an indication of how the market at large is performing.

EQUITY: The term equity can mean any number of things depending on the context, but basically it refers to the excess of assets over liabilities. Equity can also refer to the net worth of a company, or to the value of an ownership interest in a property. A stock can also be called equity because it represents ownership of a company.

FOUR PILLARS: A term used to describe the main types of financial institutions: banking, trust, insurance, and securities.

HOME EQUITY LOAN: A loan, sometimes referred to as a second mortgage, that allows owners to borrow against the equity in their homes.

INFLATION: The rise in price of goods and services. In Canada, inflation is generally measured by the Consumer Price Index (CPI).

INITIAL PUBLIC OFFERING (IPO): A company's first sale of stock to the public via a stock exchange such as the Toronto Stock Exchange (TSX). Also known as "going public."

INSIDE INFORMATION: Material information about a company that is not yet publicly available.

JUNK BOND: A bond with a high yield and a high risk. Often issued to finance a corporate takeover.

MUTUAL FUND: A special type of investment product that gives even small investors access to a well-diversified portfolio of stocks, bonds, and other securities.

NASDAQ: The National Association of Securities Dealers Automated Quotation is a computerized system in New York City that provides price quotations on over-the-counter (OTC) securities. It is the second-largest stock exchange in the U.S., in terms of the value of its securities, trailing only the New York Stock Exchange. You'll find some of the world's largest technology companies on the NASDAQ, including Amazon.com, Apple, Cisco, eBay, Google, Intel, and Microsoft. Its stock trading has always been done completely electronically.

OPTIONS: Contracts that give an investor the right, but not the obligation, to buy or sell certain securities at a specified price within a specified time.

OVER-THE-COUNTER (OTC): A security that is not listed or traded on an officially recognized stock exchange such as the Toronto Stock Exchange (TSX) or the New York Stock Exchange (NYSE).

PORTFOLIO: The group of assets held by an investor.

PROSPECTUS: A legal document that describes in detail a security being offered for sale to the public. It is an indispensable tool for determining the merit of an investment.

REGISTERED EDUCATION SAVINGS PLAN (RESP): A savings plan that allows anyone, from a parent to a family friend, to invest in a child's future education. Contributions grow tax-deferred until the child is ready to pursue a post-secondary education.

REGISTERED RETIREMENT SAVINGS PLAN (RRSP): A tax-sheltered account offered by financial institutions that allows you to save for retirement while lowering your income taxes.

S&P 500: A stock index, widely considered to be the leading indicator of the U.S. market, which consists of 500 of the largest stocks (in terms of market value).

SECURITIES: The generic term describing transferable certificates of ownership such as stocks and bonds.

SHARES: If you buy a stock you are buying a share of the company. Often used interchangeably with stocks.

SINFUL STOCK: Stock from companies that are associated with activities considered unethical or immoral such as the production of tobacco or weapons.

STOCK EXCHANGE: A stock exchange is a place where people can buy and sell shares of stock in a publicly owned company. The stock exchange helps the buyer and seller settle on a price, charging a fee for the service.

STOCK INDEX: An index that tracks the performance of stocks. Examples include the Dow Jones Industrial Average (DJIA) and the S&P 500. Also known as a stock market index.

STOCKS: Also known as shares or equities, stocks are a type of security signifying ownership in a corporation.

TAX-FREE SAVINGS ACCOUNT (TFSA): As of January 2009, Canadian banks began offering a tax-free savings account that allows customers to deposit up to $5,000 each year. The interest earned is yours tax-free. For instance, if you earn 2.7 percent interest on $5,000, the $135 earned in interest that year wouldn't be subject to tax—saving you $19.

TAX-SHELTER: Not to be confused with tax evasion, which is illegal, a tax shelter is an investment that offers tax savings such as immediate deductions, credits, or income deferral.

TORONTO STOCK EXCHANGE (TSX): Formerly known as the TSE, the Toronto Stock Exchange is Canada's largest stock exchange.

VENTURE CAPITAL: Financing aimed at helping new companies get started or reach the next level of growth. Venture capital investments are often riskier, but offer the potential for above-average returns.

Source: Chatelaine.com

START A MONEY CLUB

Money groups, where five or six friends get together once a week or month to talk through their dreams, financial challenges, and progress, are a social solution to getting back on the money track. Everybody knows how to do math, but group support gives members the impetus to change their habits.

Decide who's in. Chances are this is the first time you'll be opening up about your financial situation, so how do you decide who to divulge your entire history to? In order for the club to serve its purpose of helping you reach your goals, everyone will need to lay their finances bare, so form a group of less than 10 people so everyone has an opportunity to share. Send an email or Facebook message to recruit acquaintances, co-workers, or friends of friends—as long as they're people who will keep the details confidential and remain committed to the group.

Questions to ask before recruiting:

- Is this someone you trust?

- Does this person have goals similar to your own?

- Is this person too busy to commit to regular meetings?

- Will I be able to hold this member accountable if they don't show or are constantly late?

- If someone asks to join an existing club, do all members consent to it?

- Will this person respect the group's privacy and comments?

Your first meeting. Money clubs are all about serious fun. So at your inaugural meeting break the ice with a few cocktails—vodka and cranberry Cape Codders are an über-frugal choice—and go around the room discussing your individual goals and reasons for joining a money group. Share your short- and long-term life plans and discuss how getting into financial shape will help you realize those plans. You'll be surprised to discover the different attitudes and relationships each woman has with money—some may be in deep debt while others might never spend money on themselves. It's important to never let judgment creep in—each person will have unique circumstances.

Time it right. Chances are you won't be reviewing bank statements right away. You'll want to warm up to the other members and divvy up some responsibilities. Decide on when and where you will regularly meet. Will you meet once a week, every other week, or once a month? Who will be responsible for taking notes or bringing drinks?

Make a schedule. It's a good idea to structure your agenda with pre-researched topics. Share your unique experiences— how you got your raise or how you successfully bargained for a lower interest rate on your credit card. You can rotate who hosts and who keeps minutes.

Do your homework. It's a good idea to send each member off with a little task for the next meeting. You're more likely to stick with the group if you know they're relying on your help too. Each member can research a different topic (credit ratings, debt repayment, retirement savings, etc.) and that way you can work out your finances as a team and avoid all the research you would otherwise have to do alone. Hold each other accountable to act on the meeting's information. Your week-to-week goals can be anything from eating out less to finding the lowest cellphone plan. Your longer-term goals could include making more money, starting your own business, building retirement savings, or repaying debt.

What to bring:

- Binder or notebook to take minutes
- Appetizers
- Drinks
- Financial statements and credit card bills

Go virtual. If you're looking for the benefits of a money club, but can't get out for a night of money talk and cosmos, try a web-based alternative. For example, visit Chatelaine.com and join the conversation on our forum to find other women like you and share money tips. Ask questions. Post answers. Find out how other women handle their cash.

DEFINE YOUR GOALS

Before investing anything, you've got to decide why you are building wealth in the first place. We all have dreams. Maybe yours is to own a house, retire at 55, pay for your kids' education, or start your own business. So sit down with a pen and pad and ask yourself: what is most important to me? Prioritize.

Maybe you're saying, "Hold on. Why can't I have it all?" Well, that would be fantastic, and perhaps your job allows it, but most people's desires are grander than their paycheques and they wind up rushing into financial decisions without contemplating what they actually want to do with their money. Pick two or three areas that mean the most to you now. Once you meet those goals, you can always go back to the others and tackle them next.

Here are a few options to get you thinking:

- Contributing to your RRSP and saving for retirement while raking in tax advantages now.

- Saving for a down payment on a house or condo in an area of town you love. First-time homebuyers can even borrow against their RRSP money for the down payment under the government's Home Buyers' Plan. Just remember, you'll have to pay the loan back within 16 years and you'll lose out on tax-deferred compounding while the money is elsewhere.

- Investing in an RESP to pay for Junior's university or college while taking extra money through the government's Canada Education Savings Grant and, if you qualify, the Canada Learning Bond. Some advisors caution clients to take care of their financial future first before investing in RESPs so you're not hitting the kids up for money when you're old and grey.

- Building an emergency fund so you can weather any financial storm.

- Saving for big purchases such as a new car or a once-in-a-lifetime vacation.

INVEST TO EARN!

It happens all the time. A couple with kids and a house pinch pennies for years so they can pay down their mortgage, ward off credit card debt, *and* contribute to their RRSPs. No wonder they say they feel like they don't have a life! By simultaneously paying down debt and throwing money at investments, they're slowing down any progress they make on both fronts.

Here's a better strategy: tackle your debt first. Let's say you have a credit card with an 18 percent interest rate. If you focus on eliminating that debt, you'll be 18 percent ahead on the debt by year's end. In other words, erasing debt guarantees a much better return on your money than nearly any investment out there today. What's more, because you can carry forward your RRSP contribution room into the future, you're not missing out on your ability to pay for retirement.

Once your debts are paid off, take the money you've been paying and begin investing it again. By focusing on one goal at a time, you'll come out ahead in the end—and feel like you're finally making progress.

One word of caution about this approach to money management: once you pay off what you owe, stay out of debt or you'll be back in the same place you started. ■

HOW MUCH RISK CAN YOU TAKE?

All financial decisions come down to one word: risk. Do we invest in this mutual fund or that one? Do we pick blue chip stocks or opt for something more volatile? Considering the real possibility of losing money, is it any wonder some women experience severe stress or opt out of investing at all?

At least that's what many years' worth of surveys and studies have shown us. While men are more likely to foster their over-confident inner Donald Trump and put their money in dicey investments—one U.S. study found that male investors trade 45 percent more than women do—women are said to exhibit more risk aversion. We research investments, take our sweet time finding advisors, and ponder financial decisions longer, they say.

But apparently this wait-and-see attitude works for us: in 2009, research from Hedge Fund Research in Chicago showed that women-owned funds delivered an annual return of 9 percent, compared with less than 6 percent for all hedge funds from 2000 onward. Still, we could possibly do even better if we ditched some of our safe-playing ways in exchange for a bit more risk. At least when we're younger and our time horizon is longer.

Start by deciding how much money you can "safely" lose without dipping into your rent, food, or emergency funds, whether it's $10,000 if you're single and in the black, or $1,000 if you're knee-deep in diapers and struggling with one salary. Then start moving your money around. Try yanking some of it out of your high-interest savings account or GIC and plunking it into index funds, blue chip stocks, or other moderately risky asset. Better yet, diversify your portfolio.

And don't forget retirement. The closer you are to practicing your retirement party speech, the less risk you can afford to take. (Can you imagine saving for 25 years and losing a hundred grand because all the experts said some company's stock was a winner—and it wasn't? No. We don't want to even think about it either.) On the other side of the coin, the younger you are and the more years you have before retirement, the more comfortable you can be with growth-oriented, volatile investments such as stocks.

Here's a simple math equation you can use when trying to decide how much of your portfolio should be made up of riskier investments versus safer bets:

1. Subtract your age from 100 (or 120 if you want to be more aggressive).

2. Invest the percentage you come up with in stocks.

3. Invest the rest in bonds, GICs or whatever conservative options you prefer.

For example, if you're 35 years old, you might invest between 65 (100 minus 35) to 85 percent of your total portfolio in stocks. The remaining money gets divvied up amongst bonds and the like. Don't take these numbers too seriously though. They're just a guideline and only you know what you can afford to lose.

BIG MONEY CONCEPTS YOU CAN'T MISS

What else do you need to know before calling up a discount brokerage and buying your way into the stock market? Read on. Here is some information that will help make the road to riches less rocky and more exciting (but in a good way):

PAY YOURSELF FIRST

This is the golden rule of personal finance (and a great way to build a long-term nest egg). Before you pay your bills, buy groceries, or anything else, set aside a portion of your income and save it. The first bill you pay each month should be going to you—or at least to your brokerage, mutual fund, or retirement accounts. Have it deducted straight from your paycheque and you won't notice it's missing—or be tempted to spend it. Many people swear that by saving 10 percent of their earnings, they're able to generate tremendous wealth over the long term.

DIVERSIFICATION

Nearly all of us have heard the advice: don't put all of your eggs in one basket. The same concept—diversification—is used in investing and it is one of the most powerful investment strategies you're going to come across. Financial experts call it a tool for "managing risk" because by spreading out your money in many uncorrelated investments, chances are that most of your investments will remain up or holding steady if one or two take a nosedive.

It's not enough to simply invest in cola, drilling, and IT company stock, even if the businesses don't seem to have much in common. Instead, to decrease the odds that your investments get bashed, you'll want to put your money in different classes of investments such as bonds, stocks, real estate, and precious metals. You can further diversify your investments by hitting both the domestic and international markets.

DOLLAR-COST AVERAGING

If you're already making regular, fixed contributions to your investments you're taking advantage of the power of dollar-cost averaging. Here's how it works: when prices are high, your money buys fewer shares, and when prices are low, your money buys more. The beauty is that over time, you will probably wind up with more shares at lower prices than if you bought them all at once. It reduces your average share cost and spreads your investment risk over time. Just remember, in order for the strategy to be effective, you must continue to purchase shares when the market goes up and when it goes down.

READ YOUR PROSPECTUS AND ANNUAL REPORTS

Mutual fund companies are required to give investors information about what they're actually sinking their money into. Where will you find it? The prospectus. Before it lands at your feet with a resounding thud, this legal document is first reviewed and audited by securities regulators. Don't worry if much of what's written makes your eyes cross, though. The most valuable information—costs, performance histories, and objectives—is summarized in its first few pages. That's what you want to understand. The rest is mainly made up of monotonous legal ramblings.

Mutual funds also send out annual reports that shed light on whether the fund is doing well, or poorly. It also provides more details on the specific investments it holds. This is good information to know, not only because you'll be curious about how much money you've gained or lost, but if, for example, you prefer to stay away from "sinful stock" and the fund now invests in tobacco or weapons, you can decide to hold tight or bail out.

DO IT NOW (AND AGAIN TOMORROW)

Now we finally come to the cornerstone rule of smart saving: save early and often.

Let's consider for a moment what would happen if you started stashing away just a few dollars every week now (brown bag your lunch one day, skip the latte, and invest the savings), instead of waiting until retirement looms. You'll actually need to save less money overall. What's more, your nest egg will be bigger. By saving now, you're taking advantage of the magic of compounding.

Here's an example:

A. It was Mary's 25th birthday when she received a card in the mail from her grandmother. Tearing the envelope open as soon as she walked in the door, she discovered five crisp $100 bills and a note that simply said: "This is your first installment for your retirement savings." Mary knew her grandmother meant business—after all, she became a millionaire at 60 when her own investments paid out—so the next day Mary took the money and invested it.

But Mary didn't stop there. Every month for the next 35 years she had $200 dollars taken directly out of her bank account and deposited into her investments. (That's less than $7 a day.) The result? When Mary turned 60 she was a millionaire too.

With an initial $500 deposit, plus $200 invested every month for 35 years and a very healthy return of 11 percent, Mary held $1,004,947 when she finally needed it.

Now consider this second scenario:

B. It was Aude's 25th birthday when she received a card in the mail from her grandmother. Taking a few minutes to pull the new clothes she had just bought out of her bags, she took a seat in her kitchen and opened the envelope. Aude discovered five crisp $100 bills and a note that said: "This is your first installment for your retirement savings."

Aude held the five $100 bills in her hand. Then she opened another envelope that contained her credit card bill. Aude's card was nearly at its limit, so, praying that her grandmother would never find out, Aude hopped online and used her birthday present to pay off the bill.

For the next 20 years, Aude put off investing anything into her RRSP. There always seemed to be other, more important things requiring her money: vacations, paying the mortgage, credit card bills, and buying the kids new shoes. But then on her 45th birthday, Aude suddenly realized retirement age was coming up fast. She tracked down a financial planner to discuss what she would need to save.

To save enough for a comfortable retirement, Aude would have to invest $5,000 right away and inject $2,000 into her investments every month for the next 15 years if she wanted to have a comparable lifestyle to someone who started saving at 25. And the kicker? Even after investing so much money, Aude would still have fewer assets than the early investor would.

The lesson:

Mary: Had an initial investment of **$500** and made further payments of **$200** a month with an 11 percent return for 35 years. The outcome: **$1,004,947.**

Aude: Had an initial investment of **$5,000** and made further payments of **$2,000** a month with an 11 percent return for 15 years. The outcome: **$933,302.**

Retirement planning is important for everyone, but particularly for women. We are living longer than ever. Recent World Health Organization data suggests the average Canadian woman can expect to live until she's 83. The average man's life expectancy rate, however, is 78. So a typical Canadian woman who retires at 60 will need enough money to get her through 23 years, possibly without support. The good news? She's alive. The bad news? She could outlive her money.

But what happens if you're no longer 25 with a time horizon spread out before you like the red carpet of opportunity? Relax. Yes, it's preferable to start saving for retirement as early as possible, but there are a few things you have going for you even if you feel you've missed the boat.

Read the conventional financial wisdom and you'll find it suggests socking away at least a million dollars—or 70 to 80 percent of pre-retirement earnings—in a retirement savings plan. But hold on. Where did the intimidating sum come from, and is it even realistic?

Here's the breakdown: if your income is $60,000 per year, most number crunchers say you should be able to maintain your current lifestyle when you retire with 70 percent of that, or $42,000 (be aware that other money pooh-bahs claim the percentage is anywhere from 55 percent to 82 percent, depending on variables such as inflation or whether you sell your house when you retire). Now multiply that number by 25 years and voila. There's that million dollars. Chances are, however, you'll need less than 70 percent since you won't have mortgage payments, daycare fees, whopping grocery bills, or commuting costs. You will probably pay less income tax too.

No one is going to deny that having a million dollars kicking around in an RRIF or annuity upon retirement would be great to add to our Old Age Security and Canada/Quebec Pension Plan benefits. Yet for most Canadians, particularly women who are out of the workforce longer to take care of children, it's tough to build that kind of wealth. No wonder Statistics Canada reveals only one in six people with a pre-retirement income of $40,000 or more saves as much money as the experts recommend.

The good news is that money conventions should be treated as guidelines rather than fixed rules. How much do you need to retire on? That depends on your lifestyle. If you're a high roller, you'll need more money. If you're frugal, you'll require less. Either way, two simple rules will help keep you on track: Get out of debt. Save whatever you can.

If you tingle at the mere idea of a day at the mall, rethink slapping down your plastic so often now. Aim for a target of zero-debt by retirement. Think about it: if you're shelling out $10,000 in credit card debt each year, paying that off automatically nets you that same 10 grand in principal and a guaranteed after-tax rate of return equal to your debt's interest, say, 22 percent.

What if you're trying to decide between an RRSP or paying off the house early? Maybe you can do both. That's right. Take your RRSP refund and pay down the mortgage. By the time you retire, you'll have a free house to live in and savings too.

Furthermore, by the time you reach your mid-40s or 50s, there's a chance many of your major expenses will be gone, such as child care, and your paycheque will be larger. In other words, you'll be in a much better position to invest that $2,000 each month for 15 years than you were in your mid-20s.

YOUR BEST INVESTMENT DEALS

Now that you have a handle on some investment savings concepts and how much risk you can stomach, where should your money go? While we don't have the space here to give you detailed information about investment options, we do want to shed light on top investments that make sound financial sense—a real godsend when you have little time or inclination to fret over charts and numbers.

GO THE COUCH POTATO ROUTE

This is the essential strategy for investment newbies and the chronically time-challenged. The so-called couch potato investor buys a selection of index funds, which are a type of mutual fund that tracks the stock index (think the Canadian S&P/TSX Composite Index), and exchange-traded funds (ETFs), which are securities that trade on the stock market. Because they track the index, they contain a portion of all the stocks in that index.

One advantage is their low cost: both index funds and ETFs typically have fees of less than one percent of your purchase. By way of comparison, mutual fund fees, called management expense ratios, can go as high as 2.5 percent.

You might be thinking, these funds hold a portion of every single security on the market? You'd need a computer to track all of that. You're right. That's exactly what happens, and the upshot of all of this is that because that computer doesn't have to be paid like a person who manages the fund, those cost savings are passed down to you.

Another plus is the minimal time commitment that comes with investing this way. Fifteen or 20 minutes a year is often all it takes to keep on top of these investments. Basically, you're just along for the ride.

And the best news yet? Historically, index funds and ETFs have been shown to beat out actively traded funds over time because they don't charge high management fees. Many financial institutions offer an index mutual fund with low fees and low investment limits through a discount broker, which means you don't have to save up to invest an initial sum. Even $100 or $500 is enough to get you in the door. There are two families of ETFs to choose from in Canada: iShares and Claymore Securities.

You can find out more about how to be a couch potato investor by visiting Canadianbusiness.com.

OTHER MUTUAL FUNDS

Want to get more action than a typical couch potato? Try mutual funds for a quick road to a diversified portfolio. A mutual fund is a professionally managed investment that pools money from many investors and invests it in anything from stocks to bonds and from short-term money market instruments to other securities. The mutual fund's manager trades the pooled money regularly. If the fund does well, all of the investors are in the money. If it doesn't do well, however, they lose. Net proceeds or losses are typically distributed to investors annually.

So what do you need to consider before investing in a mutual fund? Cost, for one. The charges you pay to buy or sell a fund can have a huge impact on your rate of return. All fees are not created equal. Loads, or up-front commissions paid to brokers and financial advisors who sell mutual funds, take a bite out of your earnings too. Put it this way, if your mutual fund paid out 10 percent last year but you paid four percent in sales loads, that fabulous investment starts to seem ho-hum.

The only way to be sure you are getting a no-load fund, or at least a smaller load fund, is to look at the prospectus for the fund. Without all of the marketing hype, you'll be able to see quite clearly the fees you're actually paying. Research funds and track performance at Canadianbusiness.com.

SUSS OUT STOCKS

Now for the risky option: stocks. Do well with these investments and you could be looking at a big, fat return on your investment. Do poorly, like those crying into their Bay Street bar beer glasses during recessions, and you could lose it all. So how can you make sure you're a winner? Well, there are no guarantees, but look for stocks offered by companies with low debt, high cash levels, and seasoned management teams. If you're adverse to risk, consider blue chip stocks, such as those of banks and utilities. They tend to pay dividends and have stable returns even during market downturns.

More of a risk taker? Check out resource- and commodities-based companies like those in oil and gas. While they tend to get hit the hardest when the economy tanks, they also tend to recover the most.

Experts suggest that investing in about 20 stocks across five sectors will give you a diversified portfolio (meaning one that is made up of companies that vary in size, sector, and geography). Investing in stocks requires a commitment of several hours a week, so you can stay abreast of company news and analysts' reports that will help you decide if you're going to stay the course or sell. Knowing when to sell is the toughest call of all, so you might want to put a stop-loss order on your stocks, which means if they drop below a certain price, your online broker program will automatically sell.

THE RRSP ADVANTAGE

We'll be examining RRSPs at greater length in the following chapter, but because Registered Retirement Savings Plans offer such great benefits, we'll quickly mention them here too.

An RRSP is not actually an investment, but a way to register your investments. Think of an RRSP as an umbrella sheltering your hard-earned money from taxes. As long as these stocks, bonds, GICs, or mutual funds are registered as an RRSP, they won't get hit. At least not until you turn 71 and are required by law to terminate your RRSPs and convert them into some form of retirement income. But at that point, you might be in a lower tax bracket anyway.

Nearly any investment you can think of is deemed RRSP material.

So how many of your investment dollars can go towards an RRSP? The government's deduction limit is generally calculated as 18 percent of a person's earned income from the previous tax year minus any "pension adjustment," up to a specified maximum, plus any unused room carried forward. This specified maximum keeps rising.

WHAT'S THE MAXIMUM RRSP LIMIT?

Year	Contribution Limit
2004	$14,500
2005	$16,500
2006	$18,000
2007	$19,000
2008	$20,000
2009	$21,000
2010	$22,000

It's important to remember that even though an RRSP is usually intended for retirement, the funds can also be used to take advantage of the federal government's Home Buyers' Plan, a program that allows you to borrow up to $25,000 tax-free and interest-free from your RRSP to put toward the purchase of your first home.

INVEST TO EARN!

Quick! If someone gave you $5,000 would you:

A: Use it to pay off your mortgage faster.

B: Throw it at your RRSP and watch your tax bill shrink.

C: Put the money into a Tax-Free Savings Account (TFSA).

D: All of the above.

Decisions, decisions. With so many options since January 1, 2009, when the government launched the new Tax-Free Savings Account, what should we do with our extra money? The TFSA is a flexible investment account that allows you to sock away money—up to $5,000 per year—without paying tax on any growth. As long as you're 18 and have a Social Insurance Number, you can open one of these accounts at banks or other financial institutions.

Unlike an RRSP, it's not tax-deductible so it doesn't actually bring down the amount of tax you pay each year, but—here's the kicker—you can withdraw your money at any time and you don't pay tax on those withdrawals. You also get to keep that balance available for later. Conversely, if you take money out of an RRSP, you get dinged big time because it's considered taxable income.

But its greatest strength may also be the TFSA's most onerous impediment to saving wisely. Because a TFSA gives us access to our money whenever we need it without penalty, it could be a little too easy to deplete those funds if, say, that spiffy spring jacket in your favourite boutique window beckons. But not many people would dip into RRSP money to buy something so frivolous. The penalties alone could cost more than the coat itself.

Read the papers and you'll see that financial experts say there's no real difference in earnings potential between an RRSP and TFSA, so maybe deciding between the two has to come down to self-restraint. If you're a spender, or are in a high tax bracket and could use the immediate tax rebate, stick with an RRSP, but if you're discipline incarnate, opt for the flexibility of a TFSA. Or split the difference and use both.

Spenders and savers alike could do worse than treating their TFSA like an RRSP anyway. Some planners recommend thinking of the TFSA in terms of long-term retirement savings, not merely as a means to save up for a trip to Florida next year. RRSP and pension funds can go to funding everyday living expenses when you retire, but that $60,000 saved up in the tax-free account sure could come in handy if the refrigerator blows or the leaky roof needs to be replaced when you're 72.

KEEP IT GOING

There. Your 30 minutes are up and now you're on your way to managing your money and watching your investments build and grow for the long term. Next stop, taxes. But wait! Don't skip the next chapter. Sure, no one likes the idea of shuffling 30 percent of our income to the government, but if you stick with us, we'll show you incredibly intelligent techniques and tips to save money on taxes and avoid costly mistakes . . . no hair pulling required.

Chapter 5
GET YOUR TAX ACT TOGETHER

....

It's nine o'clock on a Monday night and Estelle is finally sneaking out of her twin daughters' room after getting them down for bed. She rubs her own tired eyes, takes a deep breath, and wanders into the kitchen. Her husband James is up to his elbows in dish water, rinsing the dinner plates and loading the dishwasher, so Estelle grabs the broom and gets busy sweeping the crumbs and pieces of fly-away food that litter the floor.

Before finally crawling into bed at midnight, there's laundry to fold, a couple of light bulbs to change, and a project from work to finish for a meeting the next day. And at the very back of Estelle's mind is one more task she better tackle soon: taxes.

"Taxes" has been on Estelle's internal to-do list forever, it seems. It's already mid-July and she knows that she has been paying interest since the April 30 tax deadline came and went over two months ago. Still, she and James never seem to get around to filing.

"We've been so busy this year with the girls and work, that we just keep putting off doing our taxes," says Estelle. "Besides, half of my receipts are in piles all over the house. I don't even know where to start."

It's not until Estelle and James receive a late-filing notice from the Canada Revenue Agency that they're spurred into action. Although they used to file taxes on their own before their busy twins arrived the year before, the couple realizes that unless they make an appointment with a professional, they'll never get around to tackling the tax tiger.

They find an accountant through a friend, book a day off work and show up with all the tax forms and receipts they can find. Four hours later, Estelle and James are done—and a little richer than they realized, even after they've paid the accountant's fee.

"Hiring her was a great idea. She found ways to save us money we'd never thought of," Estelle says.

MANY TIME-PRESSED CANADIANS FEEL MORE THAN a tinge of tedium come tax time, which no doubt contributes to the over one million late tax returns filed each year in this country. So it's not just you. Tax forms are confusing at best and infuriating at worst as elected officials make piecemeal changes to the tax codes like a house renovation project gone mad. Throw in our own busy, cluttered, and chaotic lives and is it any wonder tax season seems so dreadfully . . . taxing?

It's time to kiss any feelings of tax dread goodbye because in this chapter we're going to show you how to uncover new ways to slash the dollars you pay this year. (Trust us. It's incredibly satisfying watching the numbers creep down as you type in your child's camp fees or watch your RRSP contributions in action.) Beyond that, you're also going to find out when it's a good idea to do your own taxes versus hiring a pro, how to keep on top of your paper trail, and what to do if the taxman cometh. And don't forget RRSPs. We'll be discussing their merits in more detail here too.

DIY OR
HIRE A PRO?

When Estelle and James were younger, less frazzled, and their tax situation was more straightforward, the do-it-yourself route made a lot of sense. They simply bought tax software, gathered up their T4s and other government forms sent to them by the end of March each year, grabbed the student loan interest documents, and settled in for an evening of plunking in numbers on the computer.

But now with children, daycare costs, RRSP contributions, a new home, and James's small web design business (an offshoot of his day job), filing taxes is far more complicated—and worrisome. James and Estelle don't have the time to become tax experts so they are certain they're missing out on tax reductions and making costly mistakes.

Competent tax specialists can save them both headaches and money—sometimes so much money it's enough to make up for the fees they charge—but what kind should Estelle and James hire?

Tax professionals fall into a few categories and one is not necessarily better than the other. They simply perform different functions. For instance a tax preparer generally has the least amount of training and fewest credentials, but is a great choice for those with an uncomplicated tax situation. H&R Block, one of the best-known tax preparation companies, has offices across the country, but there are other smaller companies too. Tax preparers are the most economical choice, charging about $150 for a basic return. (By way of comparison, QuickTax software runs about $40. You can even find basic online versions for free.)

Meanwhile certified general accountants are a good economical choice for people who have moderately complicated tax returns, but who don't need handholding throughout the year. Many CGAs can help you if you're self-employed. Try to find one that has some knowledge about your industry, however, so they can be better prepared to tell you if your, say, magazine subscriptions count as a business expense. Again, straightforward tax returns will be in the hundred dollar plus range, while more complex returns will mean paying several hundred dollars.

Chartered accounts, or CAs, tend to work in larger firms such as KPMG or Ernst & Young and have the expertise to prepare complicated returns and offer in-depth advice. If you have numerous tax shelters or live in two countries and file returns in both, a CA might be a good choice, but they will cost you. The same goes for tax lawyers who work for very-high-earner types with major tax conundrums. Expect to pay hundreds of dollars an hour if you hire one.

GET YOURSELF ORGANIZED

No matter who you choose, to get the job done right your tax specialist will need you to supply forms, receipts, RRSP information, and any other material to file your taxes quickly and easily. (In other words, don't show up at her office with a grocery bag full of receipts, dump them on her desk, and say, "You figure it out." That's not how it works.) So what is she looking for?

- The previous year's notice of assessment
- Any tax amounts paid by installments
- A copy of last year's tax return (if you're a new client)
- Details of personal changes such as birth, marriage, separation
- Universal Child Care Benefit details
- Receipts for public transit passes
- Any T3, T4, or T5 forms covering employment, commissions, employment insurance, workers' compensation, Registered Retirement Income Funds, etc.
- RRSP contribution slips

- A gain/loss statement from your broker
- Charitable donation receipts
- Interest paid on student loans
- Medical, dental, nursing home, or other private medical insurance receipts
- Spousal support income/payments
- Details of your dependants and their medical status
- Child care information including receipts (for summer camp, list dates too)
- Moving expenses

Be as organized as you possibly can. Tally your invoices and other records. Clip groups of receipts together or stuff them in corresponding envelopes with the category written at the top. Accountants are often paid by the hour so the less work you make them do, the less you'll be doling out for their services. You can find a more comprehensive list of documents needed on your province's Certified General Accountants website. In Ontario, for example, visit Cga-ontario.org.

THE CASE FOR DIY

Using professionals come tax time has a lot of advantages. It's convenient, for one. They can also save you hundreds of dollars in tax deductions. But preparing your own taxes has benefits too. You're not a slave to someone else's schedule (who is very often overworked and tired leading up to April 30), and you'll be able to see first-hand how your financial decisions have an impact on the amount of tax you pay. Don't like what you see? Make new decisions next year. And don't forget tax software. Some of the best choices such as QuickTax and UFile are actually simple, use plain language, and even give you hints and tips along the way.

TAME THE PAPER TRAIL

File taxes yourself or go with a pro. No matter how you decide to pay the taxman, if you break out in a sweat just thinking about your box of crumpled receipts hiding in the closet (if they ever made it there in the first place) and a missing T4, it's time to take charge and become organized all year. These simple steps will keep you feeling calm and prepared come tax season.

BAG ON THE WALL

Pick one place in your house to hang a (big) bag on the wall, or use an accordion file, and consider that your "Tax Zone." Every time you empty your wallet, pay a bill, or receive a piece of tax material (assessment forms, your T4, etc.), chuck the papers into the bag or file. There. Done.

LABEL

Now create your system. Label each file by the appropriate tax category (transportation, RRSP contributions, charitable donations, utilities, medical expenses, daycare, etc.) and sort your receipts and papers into those categories. If you decide to use envelopes instead, take a three-hole punch to them and make them binder ready. Whatever works for you.

GO HIGH TECH

Using personal finance software is another good way to stay on top of the paper trail. Enter receipts and expenses into the fields provided each week and keep a running tab. Yes, it takes a bit of extra time now, but come April taxes will be a breeze.

DO IT OFTEN

Clear your desk and wallet of receipts regularly (say, every Sunday evening). As a result, your wallet will lose its bulge, and those receipts won't get lost or damaged by getting crunched in the bottom of your bag.

THROW IT OUT

Do you need to keep every single receipt that comes in the door? Probably not. If you know for sure you can't write off your new DVD player, keep the receipt only until the warranty expires, then toss it out. As a general rule, keep your credit card statements, T4s, RRSP contribution documents, out-of-pocket medical expenses, charity receipts, or any other tax-filing information for six years—just in case you get audited. And when you do dispose of these papers, make sure to shred them, or at least any part of them that could identify you—your name, address, SIN, etc.

TOSS THE TAX!

When we talk about a "write-off" or "writing off an expense," what does that actually mean? Here's what it doesn't mean: you're getting that item or service for free. Instead, a tax write-off means that the good or service value is deducted from your taxable income—not from the tax itself. In other words, let's say you run a small business at home and earned $60,000. You also bought $500 worth of office supplies the same year. Because they were legitimate business expenses, the deduction lowers your taxable income to $59,500 so you end up paying less in taxes depending on your tax bracket. ∎

WRITE IT OFF AND SAVE

You would never walk into a store, pick up a new belt, and offer to pay more than the sticker price, would you? So why do so many Canadians hand over more money to the government than is required each year? It's time to find ways to increase your tax deductions—anything you can subtract from your income after totalling that income and before you calculate the final damage. Here are some tax write-offs (all perfectly legal) you may have never considered that could save you hundreds or thousands of dollars this year.

RRSPs TO THE MAX

Throwing money into a Registered Retirement Savings Plan is so important that many accountants will tell you to borrow money to max out your contributions each year. Not only do RRSPs slash down the total taxes you'll pay, but by the time you withdraw the money at retirement age, you'll most likely be in a lower tax bracket so the taxes you pay on them will be smaller too. Not a bad deal. The percentage of your earnings that you can contribute to an RRSP rises each year, so check out the Canada Revenue Agency website to get the latest figures.

Want to make contributions hassle-free? Arrange for your deductions to come right off your paycheque each week or month instead of joining the bank lines and scrambling to make the deadline in February.

Just a word of caution about RRSP loans: if you are shelling out to pay off a handful of maxed-out credit cards, pay that debt down before taking on any new RRSP loan debt. You'll be getting a bigger bang for your buck.

ALL IN THE FAMILY

Every parent knows that children take a big bite out of our assets. But guess what? They can actually save you money at tax time. Submitting daycare receipts isn't the only way to save on taxes, either. You can deduct fees for lunch and after-school programs and even summer camps. If you qualify and your child is under the age of seven, you could claim up to $7,000 a year. If your child is over seven but under 16 years of age, you may be able to claim up to $4,000. There is no age limit if you have a disabled child, and you might be able to claim up to $10,000. In general, the lower-income-earning spouse makes the claim.

Or sign your kids up for soccer, yoga, or anything else that moves their bodies. The Children's Fitness Tax Credit allows parents to claim up to $500 per year of money spent on sports or fitness programs for kids under 16. (Sorry, sports equipment doesn't qualify.)

And don't forget to collect the Canada Child Tax Benefit for children living with you under the age of 18. Just remember, the more money you earn, the less the government will grant you. Still, *every* parent with kids under six is eligible for the Universal Child Care Benefit, which pays $100 per month per child. But watch out: that hundred bucks is considered taxable income (which basically means the government is doling out the equivalent of hiring a sitter one evening a month. Don't get us started . . .).

Finally, if you're providing in-home care to ageing parents or grandparents over 65, or other sick people or dependent relatives 18 and older, the Caregiver Tax Credit may be yours for the taking.

SCHOOL TAX RULES

Between tuition fees, textbooks, and their seemingly never-ending need for glue sticks (seriously, how much glue can a typical seven-year-old go through each day?), every little tax reduction you can ferret out helps. Use the textbook tax credit to get back $65 per month, or $20 for part-time scholars. And don't forget that tuition fees and education credits your child doesn't need can be used to reduce your tax load too.

BREAKS FOR CAREGIVERS

If you are caring for a sick or elderly parent, grandparent, or other disabled dependant over 18, the Caregiver Tax Credit is there for you. As long as your dependant's net claim is less than $18,081, and your maximum claim amount of $4,095 for each dependant meets requirements, you'll be able to qualify. These numbers change so check with the CRA if you have questions.

BRING IT ON HOME

The mud room roof leaked, your kitchen counter needed an upgrade, and it was time to spring for central air. Good news! Because you hired a contractor between January 27, 2009 and February 1, 2010, you may be eligible for a Home Renovation Tax Credit. At the time of this book's publication, the credit is only available for the 2009 tax year and applies to eligible expenditures of more than $1,000, but not more than $10,000. The resulting maximum tax credit equals $1,350.

So what are some examples of eligible expenses?

- Kitchen, bathroom, and basement renovations
- Windows and doors
- New carpet or hardwood floors
- New furnace, boiler, wood stove, fireplace, water softener, water heater, or oil tank
- Permanent home ventilation systems
- Central air conditioner
- Permanent reverse osmosis systems
- Septic systems
- Wells
- Electrical wiring in the home (e.g., changing from 100 amp to 200 amp service)
- Solar panels and solar panel trackers
- Painting the interior or exterior of a house
- Building an addition, garage, deck, garden/storage shed, or fence
- Re-shingling a roof
- Building a new driveway or resurfacing a driveway

- Exterior shutters and awnings
- Permanent swimming pools (in-ground and above ground)
- Permanent hot tub and installation costs

That's right. Hot tubs. (For a longer list of eligible expenses, visit the CRA's Home Renovation Tax Credit website at Cra-arc.gc.ca/hrtc.)

So are there any housing-related expenses that are *not* eligible? Yes. Ongoing maintenance fees for services such as snow removal, lawn care, pool cleaning, and monthly security bills are not included. You can't claim carpet cleaning or window washing either. And your housecleaner? You might consider her a permanent fixture in your life, but sorry. The government isn't going to pick up the tab.

Caution: make sure that the person you hired to do your renovations is legit (i.e., wasn't expecting you to pay in cash under the table), or you won't have the files and invoices needed to make a claim. In addition, if you hired Uncle Larry to install new windows, the work is ineligible unless it meets all other requirements and you can prove he is registered for the goods and services tax/harmonized sales tax under the Excise Tax Act.

And don't forget the ecoENERGY Retrofit program that provides homes and properties up to $5,000 for energy improvements. Go green, save green. Visit Ecoaction.gc.ca for more information.

MONEY FOR HOME NEWBIES

Did you buy your first house in 2009 or do you plan to in subsequent years? First-time homebuyers, and those who have not owned or lived in another home for the four preceding years, can take advantage of the Home Buyers' Tax Credit (HBTC), a non-refundable tax credit, as long as their closing date for the qualifying home was after January 27, 2009. The HBTC—meant to help with closing costs such as legal fees and property transfer taxes—is calculated by multiplying the lowest personal income tax rate for the year by $5,000. For example, because the lowest rate was 15 percent in 2009, the credit that year is $750.

If you have a disability or are buying a home for a relative with a disability, you do not have to be a first-time homebuyer. Remember, though, that you must be buying the house or condo to have a more accessible living space, or because it makes it easier to care for the person with the disability.

MOVE IT

Packing, sorting, and hauling boxes out to the truck. Moving is time-consuming and stressful, but at least you can count on some major tax breaks for your trouble. If you relocated at least 40 km to start a new job or business, you can deduct storage, transportation, and even the costs associated with cancelling and old lease. What you can't write off: any losses from the sale of your old home or the cost for moving a mobile home. (But if you have furniture in it when it's being moved, you can write off what it would have cost you to move it by going the U-Haul route. Go figure.)

COMMUTING PAYS

Next time you're standing on a packed subway platform with a thousand other commuters, take a deep breath (just not too deep) and remember you can claim your monthly public-transit pass on your tax return. Keep your receipt when you buy a monthly (or longer-duration) pass for subways, busses, streetcars, commuter trains (including VIA, as long as you hop the train to get to work), and even local ferries, and you can deduct the cost of your commute and receive money back.

IT'S A MEDICAL MIRACLE

When was the last time you claimed a medical expense? Never? According to some experts, not claiming medical expenses is the number-one tax break we miss out on. Maybe you never bothered to make a claim because the minimum required is quite steep (the total amount of receipts must exceed $1,844 or three percent of net income, whichever is less) or you assumed your prescriptions for eyeglasses wouldn't count. But what you might not realize is how many medical expenses are on the CRA list. Think ambulance rides, contact lenses, laser eye surgery, hearing aids, orthopaedic shoes, a breast prosthesis, pacemakers, and tutoring services for someone with a learning disability. Even an air conditioner—so long as it's for a patient with a severe chronic ailment, disease, or disorder—makes the cut.

You can claim any expenses that weren't eligible under or paid out by your company's benefit plan, providing you have a prescription. For example, your plan covers $300 for physical therapy per annum, but you spent $1,500 after a skiing accident last winter. You can deduct the remaining $1,200 you spent on treatments.

Plus, all the fees you paid into health and dental premiums last year may be claimed.

Still don't think you qualify? Keep in mind that you can claim expenses in any 12-month period ending in the tax year you're filing in—July 2008 to June 2009, for instance— so maximize the credit and pick a time when those expenses added up.

COMBINE CHARITABLE RECEIPTS

He gave $100 to his boss so she could run for the cure. You wrote a $150 cheque to help disadvantaged kids go to camp. This year, pool your charitable donation receipts and claim them on one return to enjoy a bigger tax break. The first $200 you claim grants you a 15.5 percent tax credit, but everything after that racks up 29 percent.

BE YOUR OWN BOSS

Your dollhouse decorating hobby earns you a tidy little sum each year. Guess what? Even if you toil as a corporate executive during the day, that sideline hobby is a business—and you can use it to write off a huge array of expenses including house mortgage insurance, utilities, and property taxes. Just be sure you have proof that you at least intend to sell your wares, whether that means holding onto a receipt for your online ad banner or keeping sales letters you sent by email.

Don't forget to pay the kids or a lower-earning spouse a salary for stuffing envelopes, answering phones, or maintaining your little company's website. You can deduct that salary against your income, save on taxes, and still keep the money in the family.

TOSS THE TAX!

Feeling smug because your friends are all scrambling to find money to pay the government on April 30 and you're sitting pretty with a big, fat refund? Bad news. A tax refund might seem preferable to pushing a wad of money over to the feds each year, but your money-back deal is no deal at all. It simply means you overpaid in taxes last year and while the government has been enjoying your interest-free loan, it could have been working for you. (Unless, of course, you've got your RRSP contribution to thank for the windfall.)

If you've been paying too much income tax each year, it might be time you ask your employer for a form to decrease the amount of taxes lopped off your paycheque. Better still, use the money you're retaining each month to pay down your mortgage faster or wipe out other debts. ■

RRSP 1, 2, 3

Let's pretend the end of February is in sight. With the cut-off date for contributing to your RRSPs approaching, what are you doing to prepare?

    A.   Scrambling like a mad woman to gather funds and take out an RRSP loan.

    B.   Sitting in the Florida sunshine and relaxing. You have a plan that automatically invests money in your RRSP each month. Who's worrying?

    C.   Nothing. No money. No time.

It's amazing how many otherwise smart, savvy women wait until the last minute to invest or forgo investing in Registered Retirement Savings Plans at all. After all, the government is practically paying you to save your money and take control of your future!

As we mentioned before, an RRSP isn't an investment, per se, but a *way* to register your investments that shelters your money from taxes and allows those funds to grow tax-free until you withdraw them upon retirement. And don't forget the tax deduction. Depending on your tax bracket, you can save up to 40 percent on your taxes through your contribution. So, a $1,000 contribution to your RRSP can reduce your tax bill by up to $400.

What's not to love?

Virtually any and all investments can be housed under the RRSP umbrella today. That's the good news. There are a few words of caution we need to mention, however, since some investment vehicles make better financial sense than others. For instance, stay away from annuities. They allow investment dollars to compound without being taxed—but isn't that what your RRSP does already? Why bother double-dipping in the same water hole? Besides, annuities carry higher annual operating expenses and reduce your earnings.

Limited partnerships are a bad bet too for many of the same reasons, plus it's often tough to get your money out of them come retirement.

So what sort of investments should you place under your RRSP umbrella? Again, that depends on how much risk you're willing and able to take, your investing personality, the current economy, and when you need the cash. Here's a short chart outlining some popular choices, their level of risk, and whether they make it easy to get your money out when you need it.

RRSP investment type	Level of risk	Easy to liquidate?
Savings account	Low	Yes
Money market funds	Low	Yes
GICs and term deposits	Low	No
Canada Savings Bonds	Low	Yes
Mortgage funds	Medium	Yes
Mortgages	Medium	Not always
Bonds	Medium	Not always
Balanced funds	Medium	Yes
Stocks (Cdn. and foreign)	Medium/High	Yes
Precious metals funds	Medium/High	Yes

Remember, although some of these options look like a good bet—they're less risky and their liquidity can't be beat—they can make for poor RRSP choices because their earnings are far too low. Some of them, such as savings accounts and money market funds, don't even keep up with inflation! Meanwhile, balanced mutual funds—particularly no-load funds that avoid paying costly commissions—offer a good middle-of-the-road option for those who want to diversify and who feel comfortable taking on some risk. Again, the younger you are and the longer time horizon you have, the more risk you can shoulder with a portfolio strong with equity (i.e., stocks or shares of a company, precious metals funds).

Whichever option you choose to invest in, there are a few RRSP rules that will help make the process easier and more lucrative in the long term.

DO IT NOW

Yes, we're back at the main tenet of financial planning—make sure you put money aside for savings *every month*. That way, when RRSP season rolls around, you won't be clambering to find money to put away. Set up an automatic transfer to your RRSP on a monthly basis—whether it's $50 or $500, every little bit helps!

MAX OUT

If you can, try to maximize your contribution—the limit for 2009 is the lesser of either 18 percent of your earned income or $21,000. Want to know what this year's contribution limit is? Check last year's notice of assessment—it's written there in black and white—or contact the CRA.

PAY IT FORWARD

If you don't max out your RRSP contribution this year, then the "deduction room" is carried forward to future years. Assume a taxpayer makes a contribution of $10,000 for 2009, even though her contribution limit is $21,000. The unused deduction "room" of $11,000 can be carried forward indefinitely and added to the calculation of the next year's deduction limit.

LEAVE IT ALONE

No matter how tough times get, try not to dip into your RRSP savings. Not only will you probably pay whopping penalties, but when you withdraw that money, 100 percent of it will be taxable today. Ouch! Instead, focus on building up a reserve of cash in your portfolio to help you out on a rainy day. Ideally, it would be great to have enough to replace your income, if necessary, for at least six months, but three months is a good starting point.

TOSS THE TAX!

So you've filed your taxes, received your assessment form, and everything is in order until next year. But what's this crumpled up in your pocket? An old receipt for a monthly transit pass? A restaurant bill for that dinner where you wooed a new client into signing with you? Maybe a charitable receipt you forgot about?

Don't be tempted to dump it in the trash. You can still claim some receipts even after the official filing date has passed. Here's how: visit the Canada Revenue Agency at Cra-arc.gc.ca, log into "My Account," and choose "Change My Return." Follow the directions and you'll be able to add those wayward receipts to your most recent income-tax return and those of the previous two years. Need to go back in time even further? You can. Up to 10 years into the past. You'll just have to mail in the changes instead. ■

WRITE-OFFS FOR
THE SELF-EMPLOYED

If you run your own businesses or work solo as a freelancer, buckle up—because you can enjoy even more tax reduction perks. But you'll also face more headaches: keeping track of receipts for printer toner, raw materials costs, coffee with clients, gas, and car maintenance fees. (The upside? You can write most of these off.) You, more than anyone else, must have some tax receipt system.

And here's one more piece of advice: look at all of your receipts each and every week, and write down—either on the receipt itself or by using personal finance software—what they were for. Waiting weeks or months later to do this job is a nightmare. Also, ensure the receipts show what they're for, as well as having a legible vendor's name and date.

But what makes a business expense legit? That's easy. In order to determine if something is truly a tax-busting business expense, ask yourself: "Would I have bought this particular item if I wasn't in business?" Of course some expenses fall into a grey area. A freelance writer and copyeditor would certainly buy pens and pencils for home use, but she also needs them for work. If you're really worried about being audited, save receipts for home pens and work pens. If you get audited about your footloose-and-fancy-free pen buying ways, you'll have proof you're only writing off those used in the office.

Here is a short list of business write-offs you'll want to consider in April or by June 15, when businesses must file their tax returns:

- Belong to a professional association? Write off your annual membership dues.

- Interest you pay toward loans to run your business are tax deductible. For more information on this tax deduction, see the "Interest" section of the CRA's Business and Professional Income guide.

- Deduct the premiums you pay for insurance on buildings, machinery, or equipment you use to run your business.
- Don't forget bank fees. That $120 a year you pay just to have a chequing account is tax deductible.
- Surprise; supplies! Those pens, paper, paper clips, staplers, and sticky-notes can really add up over the course of a year. If you're a photographer working with old-school film, write the rolls off. If you're a vet, animal drug expenses can reduce your taxes too.
- Deadbeat clients get written off in more ways than one. If someone hasn't paid you in the previous year, state that on your tax forms as a business expense.
- Legal and accounting services are tax deductible.
- Entertainment. Did you pay for tickets to send a favourite client to a hockey game? Or maybe you just picked up the cheque at a business lunch. As long as these expenses were work related, they're included and you can write off 50 percent of the cost. Just remember to keep your receipts.
- Business gifts. Last December you sent all of your favourite clients gift cards to thank them for their business. That's a write-off.

Your home is your castle—and it can reap serious tax savings:

- A portion of your mortgage or rent. Let's say you own an eight-room home, for example, and two rooms are used for your business. You can write off 25 percent of your home's mortgage, rent and maintenance costs such as heat, electricity, or water, and even some cleaning supplies and toilet paper (everyone takes bathroom breaks during the workday, no?). Don't forget house insurance, either.

- Repairs done around the home where you conduct your business. That doesn't mean you can remodel your kitchen and call it a business expense—unless you're a recipe tester and the current kitchen is unusable—but if your home office needs a new coat of paint, slap it on and write it off.

- Technology used for your business. You can write off at least a portion of your Internet fees (chances are you're doing non-work related surfing too) and other software.

- Travel expenses. If you travel for your business, you can deduct travel costs including oil, licence and even registration fees. Keep a journal in your car and use it to write down mileage and gas usage when you hit the road to see a client. Don't forget parking meter fees as well.

TOSS THE TAX!

Until recently, if you bought a new computer for work, you wouldn't have been able to deduct the entire cost of it on your income tax that year. Instead, you used the Capital Cost Allowance, or CCA, to deduct a portion of it as an income tax deduction and continued doing this over a period of years as the computer depreciated.

But that changed in 2009 when the government introduced a temporary 100 percent CCA rate for computers acquired after January 27, 2009 and before February 1, 2011, allowing us to fully expense our investment in computers in just one year instead of spreading it out over several years. ■

WHAT IF I FILE LATE?

Miss the tax deadline? Here's what you pay: If you file after April 30, tack on an extra five percent of your outstanding balance to your total. So if you owe $5,000, that's a whopping $250—even if you file the very next day, May 1.

And don't forget other costly penalties. If your Canadian income tax is in arrears, the Canada Revenue Agency will also whop you with a penalty equalling one percent of the balance owing for each full month that your return is late, to a maximum of 12 months. And that's only if you haven't been charged a late-filing penalty in the previous three years. Repeat offenders can be expected to cough up 10 percent of the balance owing for the current year and two percent of the balance owing for each full month the current income-tax return is late—to a maximum of 20 months.

Sometimes, however, life gets in the way and doing taxes runs a distant third or fourth place on a person's priority list. While you'll never be able to negotiate the *amount* of tax you owe the government, some situations warrant flexibility when it comes to figuring out interest and penalties.

If there has been a serious illness or death in the family, if you've lost your job, if there was a fire at your house, or if you experienced other circumstances beyond your control, you may be able to get the CRA to reduce or cancel the penalties you would normally owe due to late filing. The agency may even set up extended filing deadlines or a payment plan to take some of the stress off you.

No matter what the reason for filing a late tax return, you have options. Call the Canada Revenue Agency at 1-800-959-8281 and talk to an agent. Plead your case. If you take the time to connect, you and the agent can work out a repayment plan. Visit the CRA website to find the "Request for Taxpayer Relief" form RC4288.

WHEN THE AUDITOR COMES TO CALL

Having an audit notice land on the doorstep is enough to make even the most cool and collected taxpayer raise her face to the heavens and wail, "Why me?"

Breathe.

Getting audited is usually not the nightmare you would expect it to be.

Perhaps the problem with the auditing process is that it makes people feel they're being accused of a crime or trying to beat the system. In reality, if you've made this year's audit list, there's a good chance you're there simply because you've been randomly selected. Random audits help the CRA find common areas where mistakes are made. Or perhaps your file came up in someone else's audit. And some people are simply more likely to be audited than others, such as the self-employed, salespeople, or anyone else who is often paid a portion of their earnings in cash.

Of course sometimes an audit is booked when agents notice inconsistencies in your forms, you've claimed abnormally large deductions compared to other years, or someone has tipped off the government that you're evading taxes. (Think disgruntled employee or ex-spouse.)

Whatever you do, though, don't ignore the audit request letter. Preparing for an audit isn't so bad, especially if you have kept receipts and notes for the past six years in a convenient location.

Here's something else you might not have realized: if you're audited, the CRA informs you which portions of your tax return it wants to scrutinize. You're not going to be asked to pull out years and years of documents and paper piles. Trust us. They have no interest in wading through all of that stuff either. So when it comes time to talk to your auditor, remember to discuss only the portions of the return he or she wants to see.

Now is not the time to get nervous and start blabbing about other items not on the table—or you'll run the risk of opening a whole new Pandora's Box.

If you hired a tax professional, such as a certified general accountant, to prepare your original tax documents, you'll probably ask that person to represent you during the audit process. Not only has she been through this before with other clients, she'll be able to talk the talk with the auditor. Even though you'll be paying her for the service, she'll probably save you prep time, stress, and money. (Because don't forget, the auditor's job is to find more money for the CRA.)

That being said, remember that an auditor is a person just doing his or her job. So treat them with respect even if you're not fond of what they have to say. Don't argue; state your case and move on. If you feel you've been bamboozled, there are plenty of bureaucratic layers of government folks to plead your case to. You can even take your case to court if all else fails.

TOP TIPS TO AVOID AN AUDIT

- File on time.
- Use a tax specialist or computer software so you don't make math errors.
- Declare all of your income.
- If you run a business, don't declare losses year over year. At some point you should start to make money.
- Send your tax forms by snail mail (some accountants swear by this).
- Declare all income, especially if you're self-employed.
- Be honest, but don't be afraid of deductions because you're worried about being audited. If you have questions or doubts about a write-off, call CRA or an accountant and ask.

Speaking of getting personal, here's a tax tip you've probably never considered: tell your story. Most tax filers assume they have to stick to the forms the government gives them. That's true up to a point. But you can also send along anything else if you think it will give the CRA agents a better picture of your finances. (This works best if you're submitting by snail mail.) And yes, that includes typing out a simple document outlining where your money went.

Maybe you're self-employed and had a baby last year so your earnings fell dramatically, but you still had to pay your business's telephone bills, utilities, and rent. Explain that. Or you've always given large amounts to charity in the past, but this year you had to hold back and plan to pool your charitable contributions with next year's numbers. Explain that too. By writing down your story clearly without a lot of fanfare, you look like you have nothing to hide.

NOT AS TAXING AS YOU EXPECTED

Alright, you're still not exactly *excited* about filing taxes, but now that you see the tax process is hardly intimidating, let's keep moving along.

Speaking of which, in the next chapter you're about to discover home buying, selling, and owning secrets that will save you money, make you money, and put you on the path to living in your dream home sooner than you ever thought possible. Ready?

Chapter 6

MORTGAGE SWEET MORTGAGE

. . . .

It's 4:45 in the afternoon and Laisha's day is winding down at work, so she stashes her files away and hops online to peruse MLS home listings. That's when she spots it—a three-storey red-brick home with a loft and backyard landscaping to die for. She quickly sends her husband the link and within minutes he shoots back a message: "Let's check it out."

The house is missing a fireplace and a gourmet kitchen—two "must haves" on Laisha's list—but it's still a gorgeous home, helped by its new paint job and luxe furniture. And after their initial walkthrough, the couple is impressed.

"Downtown houses like this don't come on the market very often. You'll want to jump on it," advises the new agent they'd found when calling the real estate company about the house.

But bells are ringing for Laisha. For starters, there's no real play space for the kids, so all their toys will have to be stored in the living room or in their bedrooms. And in order to reach the stairs to the loft where the couple wants their home office, they'll have to walk through the third bedroom. In the end, the prime location wins them over, and now they're living with the decision to buy.

"I should have checked in with my gut," says Laisha five years later. "If we had just taken our time, done some more research, and questioned everything our agent said, I'm sure we would be in a much more appropriate house for our family now. It turned out there were a lot of other similar houses in this neighbourhood going for a better price."

When she thinks about her friend Jean's home fiasco, however, she knows it could be worse.

Jean also got swept up in a well-staged home that promised a lifestyle brimming with backyard parties and homemade cookies. So much so, that even when her home inspector took her aside and said, "The basement has two dehumidifiers. That tells me we're looking at water issues," she reasoned with herself that she didn't plan to use the basement much anyway. As it turned out, a virtual river swept through the basement rooms, and although the dehumidifiers ran night and day, after a few months Jean had to cover her mouth every time she went to throw laundry in the washer. Mould covered entire swaths of drywall.

What did the previous owner's notes say about the issue? ". . . some moisture in basement."

The new house wasn't the only problem, however. Selling her previous home also turned out to be a nightmare when Jean discovered the real estate lawyer she had used botched the legal papers associated with the house purchase. She did not have a clear title on the house—meaning that she didn't legally own the property and that it wasn't completely free of claims. When this issue came to light, the lawyer wouldn't return phone calls or email. Finally she retained the bank's attorney and got the mess straightened out, but at great cost: Jean paid thousands of dollars in legal fees.

W HETHER YOU'RE LOOKING FOR A FIVE-AND-A-HALF on the Plateau in Montreal, a sweet semi-detached in Regina, or a suburban four-bedroom home near Burnaby, real estate horror stories like these are enough to make anyone's skin crawl. Between bidding wars in hot markets, languishing homes in soft ones, and fretting over mortgage terms, amortization periods, and variable rates, it's a wonder anybody moves at all.

But buying a new home can be exciting and fun if you teach yourself to find the best deals and learn how to avoid the pitfalls. Flinging around terms such as "encroachment" or "total debt service ratio"—and actually understanding them—not only gives you a confidence boost, but also helps you make better financial decisions that will save you money and headaches on the largest investment you'll likely ever make: your home.

In this chapter, we're going to give you straight facts to help you to decide when it's the right time to buy, and tools and useful advice to use during the home-buying process—not to mention rookie mistakes to avoid. We're also going to answer some of your most pertinent finance questions and offer tricks straight from the pros so you can sell the home you own in record time. (Spoiler alert: stop baking cookies and lighting cinnamon-scented candles before the open house. Slap a coat of paint on your basement's cement floor instead.) If you are already paying a mortgage on your home and have no plans to move right now, flip ahead a few pages to find out how to pay down your mortgage faster and save thousands of dollars—without spending the next five years living off mac and cheese.

It's time to kick any real estate inhibitions to the curb and make smart financial decisions about where you're going to live and how you're going to fund it.

And yes, you *can* try this at home.

APPRAISE THIS!

If you look at home ownership to give you a sense of financial security, a private space of your own, and a backyard to lounge around in, you're in good company. A Women and Home Ownership Poll released by TD Canada Trust tells us these are the three main reasons women give for purchasing a home independently, without a husband or partner in sight.

What factors impact our decision to choose one home over another? In order, they are:

1. Cost
2. Neighbourhood and location
3. Security and safety
4. Proximity to work
5. Closeness to family

So let's assume you've found an affordable home in a convenient location. Should you jump on it? Not so fast. According to this list, safety and security are obviously important.

When comparing kitchen backsplashes and guest rooms, remember to also consider what's outside. Drive around the neighbourhood at night or grab a friend and walk it together. How do you feel? Are there enough street lights and do they work? Is the home close to crime-ridden neighbourhoods? For increased safety, look for houses with attached garages and electronic garage door openers so you can walk right into your home during dark winter evenings. And remember to check the doors, locks, and windows (single-pane are easier to break than double-pane) as well. Condos above the first floor are a safer bet since most burglars want to avoid elevators. ■

ARE YOU READY TO BUY?

"Should I rent or own?" That's the question many of us ask ourselves when hitting some of the big milestones such as getting married, landing a good job, or having a baby. So what are the very first steps you should take before finding and buying a perfect pad? Consider these:

PLAY 20 QUESTIONS

Any decision about home ownership should begin with a meticulous self-analysis. Ask yourself: Where do I want to be in two years? Do I plan to have children? Do I plan to have *more* children, or are they ready to head off to school in a few years? Is there a possibility that I might be transferred to another city? How is my parents' health? Will they need to move in with me someday? Try to get a handle on the future so you know what type of living arrangement you'll be aiming for.

GIVE CREDIT TO CREDIT

Get a copy of your credit history. If your FICO scores hover in the lower range, it is time to get a firmer grasp on paying bills on time and managing your current debt load. The less debt you have, the better mortgage rate the lender will give you. So plan ahead and increase your numbers well before finding an agent and dreaming of open concept living rooms.

CRUNCH SOME NUMERALS

Now it's time to figure out how much you can possibly afford for a down payment and mortgage. You can start by calculating your net worth by subtracting your total liabilities from your total assets. It will help you find out exactly how much debt you have versus how much money you've stowed away. You'll definitely want to be in the black before ever thinking about buying a home.

Dig even deeper and tabulate your gross debt service ratio, or GDS. In basic terms, the GDS means how much of your income you can safely put toward housing costs such as principal, interest, tax, and heating without turning your castle into a poorhouse. Many home finance experts say the trick is to stay under 32 percent of your annual income. In other words, if you gross $100,000 each year, you should pay out no more than $32,000 to live in your home. Someone with that kind of income, minimal debt and with $35,000 saved up for a down payment might expect to be approved for a home ranging in price from about $350,000 to $425,000. Total debt obligation, once you factor in other loans, should not exceed 40 percent of your gross income—so if you're already paying out a large chunk of your income to car or student loans, this is probably not the best time to buy a house or condo.

Visit Canada Mortgage and Housing Corporation at Cmhc-schl.gc.ca to see how the numbers work out for you.

WHEN RENT IS BEST

Obviously, renting a property gives you more flexibility than locking yourself into a mortgage, so think long and hard before deciding to jump in and join the homebuyer's club. For some people, even when they have the money, renting just makes more sense while waiting for more job security, padding savings, or paying down debt. But if you're an unattached gal holding out for marriage before taking on a mortgage, it's time to rethink this strategy. Many other Canadian women have. According to Royal LePage Canada, 37 percent of never-married women and 45 percent of divorced or separated women own their homes.

Still, don't feel you've missed the boat if you're still renting while most of your friends are knocking out walls to renovate or picking paint chips to coat their shutters. According to TD Canada Trust's Women and Home Ownership Poll, it turns out that women purchase their first homes at all ages in Canada: 37 percent buy between ages 18 to 29, 30 percent do the deed between ages 30 to 39, and 33 percent become home-owners at 40 or above.

GET YOUR MONEY TOGETHER

So you know what you're worth and how much money you're able to spend on home ownership each month. You've also determined that it's an excellent time in your life to buy. All you need now is a down payment, which typically ranges from five to 25 percent of the total value of the home. Most people pay for it by cashing in their savings or the proceeds from the sale of a home they already own.

The rules for saving for a down payment are like any other: pay yourself first. Flip back to Chapter 2 and revisit all of the creative ways you can slash your spending. Figure out how much you can scrimp and save each month and set up automatic payments into a high-interest savings account or money market account every month. Think slow and steady. This is not the time to sink your down payment dollars into risky stock investments hoping to make enough to buy a new house quickly.

You can also ask parents, relatives, and friends for a cash gift. Mortgage lenders will not allow you to take money from them in the form of a loan, however.

Finally, first time homebuyers and those who haven't owned a house in five years have another option that helps with a down payment and shelters the money from the taxman too: the federal government's Home Buyers' Plan, or HBP, a program that allows you to borrow up to $25,000 from your RRSP to put toward the purchase of your first home.

To qualify for the HBP (and pull your RRSP money out early without incurring penalties) all of the following conditions must apply:

- You enter into a written agreement (offer of purchase) to buy or build a qualifying home. The agreement may be with a builder or contractor, or with a Realtor or private seller. Obtaining a pre-approved mortgage does not satisfy this condition.
- You intend to occupy the qualifying home as your principal place of residence.
- You don't already have an outstanding HBP balance on January 1 of the year of the withdrawal.
- Neither you nor your spouse or common-law partner owns the qualifying home more than 30 days before the withdrawal.
- You are a resident of Canada.
- You buy or build the qualifying home before October 1 of the year after the year of withdrawal.

Once you withdraw the money from your RRSP to put toward your down payment, the clock is ticking for you to pay that loan back. But here's the great news: you have 15 years to get the job done, meaning that even if you take out the full $25,000, you're on the hook for less than $200 per month. Your first repayment is due the second year following the year in which you made your withdrawals. To keep track of your payments, you will receive a Home Buyers' Plan Statement of Account each year with your tax notice of assessment or notice of reassessment. This statement will show the total HBP withdrawals, the amounts you have repaid to date, your HBP balance, and the amount you have to contribute to your RRSP and designate as a repayment for the following year.

So if you're thinking about buying your first home, should you take advantage of the HBP or simply put money aside in a house-buying fund? For many people, the HBP is a great opportunity to buy a house for a lower cost and build retirement savings too.

Here's why: although your RRSP investment will obviously grow at a slower rate since you're taking away money that is earning compound interest for your retirement, you're still winning because of that all-important larger down payment. The more money you can gather at first, the less you'll pay in interest in the long run. (And don't forget that we're talking tax-free money here.) The HBP can also get you into the housing market sooner, so that by the time you retire there's a better chance your home is paid off and you can top up your retirement savings.

For more information about the HBP, visit the Canada Revenue Agency's website and download Guide RC4135.

However you decide to cobble together a down payment, try to save up as much as you can. The larger the down payment, the less your home will cost in the end. Not only will you pay less in compound interest, but a down payment between five and 19.99 percent of one's mortgage is deemed "high-ratio" and is subject to Canada Mortgage and Housing Corporation (CMHC) insurance premium, calculated as a percentage of the loan. That premium ranges from .50 percent to seven percent. A down payment of 20 percent or greater is called "conventional" and is not subject to any premiums, so it's cheaper in the long run.

GET A HEAD START

The down payment is in the bank and it's time to go rent-free. If you're serious about looking for a new home, it's not a bad idea to approach your financial institution and find out if it will pre-approve your mortgage loan, up to a predetermined amount, before you start knocking on doors. Since you go through the same process for a traditional mortgage as for one that is pre-approved, it makes sense to do it early in the game—particularly in a hot market when sellers are looking for hassle-free offers and a sure thing.

Pre-approved mortgages have other benefits too: you're protected from rising interest rates for as long as the pre-approved mortgage applies (typically from 30 to 120 days). You also know your price limit.

Just remember that even with a pre-approval you'll still have to jump through a few more hoops to secure the mortgage. Although most of the paperwork is completed, the bank will still do a full financial check on you and look at the market value of the property. So once you're approved, don't make any changes to your financial picture until the mortgage is signed. Changing a job, buying a new car, or throwing a luxury cruise on the credit card could jeopardize the deal.

MORTGAGES AND YOU

Now that you know you're a candidate to get a mortgage, which kind should you go for? Fixed or variable? Open or closed? One with a seven-year term or the one that is only two? To recap, here are the five main elements that make up any mortgage:

1. The principal—the loan's amount.

2. The interest—what the mortgage lender charges you to borrow.

3. Blended payments—the regular payments you make to pay down the mortgage. A portion of your money goes toward the principal and the other pays the interest.

4. The amortization period—the actual number of years it will take to pay back your mortgage loan.

5. The term—the period of time you agree to make payments under specific conditions.

Let's look at variable-rate versus fixed-rate mortgages first.

Fixed-rate. Sign on for a fixed-rate mortgage, whether it's for six months or 15 years, and you will know exactly what you will be paying each and every month for the term's length because you're locking in to a fixed interest rate. If the rates go up, you will still pay the lower price. If they go down, however, you'll miss out on the discount. Many people like fixed rates because they want to avoid any surprises and they're willing to pay for that security—especially if predictions point to higher prime rates down the road.

Variable-rate. Do you like to live on the edge and possibly save money? A variable-rate mortgage might be the best choice for you. Put simply, your mortgage rates track the bank's prime rate. When it goes up, more of your money goes to paying the interest. But when the prime rate tumbles, you pay a larger portion of your principal—so you'll be mortgage free sooner. What's more, some mortgages allow you to lock in to a fixed rate at any time and stay at that rate until the mortgage term ends. Some banks offer more flexible options, so shop around.

So, fixed or variable? You know yourself better than anyone. Can you stomach the dips and sways of a variable mortgage? Or do you prefer to know exactly what your money is doing each month? If you do decide to go with a fixed mortgage, just keep in mind what Moshe Milevsky, an associate professor of finance at the Schulich School of Business at York University in Toronto, found when he ran the numbers between 1950 and 2000. He concluded consumers would be better off, on average, with a short-term variable rate mortgage, instead of a long-term fixed rate mortgage. In fact, a consumer with a $100,000 mortgage and an amortization period of 15 years would have paid $22,000 more in interest by locking in and renewing at the five-year rate instead of borrowing at prime and renewing each year. The past few years in particular have been especially kind to those who have gone the variable rate route.

You'll also want to consider open and closed mortgages in order to get the best deal.

An **open mortgage** allows you to prepay some, or all, of your outstanding mortgage balance at any time without penalty. That's fantastic news for anyone with extra money to spare, since paying off an extra $500 or $750 a year for the first five years can chop thousands of dollars off your mortgage over the long run. Many open mortgages have six-month or one-year term options and charge higher interest rates, but if you're going to pay off your mortgage faster anyway, paying a slightly higher interest rate in the short term can still be worth it. **Closed mortgages**, however, are usually offered in terms ranging from six months to 10 years and are more stringent in their prepayment options.

PAYMENT THROUGH THE AGES

Finally, what amortization period should you shoot for? It's traditional to pay off a house in 20 or 25 years, but it makes much more sense to opt for a shorter amortization time. Here's the proof: Say you have a $200,000 mortgage at six percent interest. With a 25-year amortization period, your monthly payment would be $1,279.61—equalling total payments of $383,883 over the 25-year life of your mortgage.

Now let's imagine you shorten the amortization period to 20 years so your monthly payment increases to $1,424.38. "Ugh! A bigger payment?" you say? Hold on. Because you are now only paying for 20 years, instead of 25, you have just reduced your total payments from $383,883 over 25 years to $341,851 over 20—and saved almost $42,000 over the course of your loan.

Knock off another five years and your monthly payment would be $1,679.77, but your total payments over 15 years would come in at only $302,359, for a savings of over $81,000.

If you can find another $300 or $400 a month and use it to pay your mortgage, not only will you be home-free faster, you'll have more money to spend on vacations, cottages, or anything else you want to experience . . . before your golden years.

LOCATE AN AGENT

The down payment is ready and you've decided on a mortgage type. All that's left is finding a new place to live. But buying a home for the first time—and even the fourth time—can be intimidating. How do you know if you're paying a fair price? Should you walk away from a sale if it turns out that that gorgeous old home is wired basement to attic in knob and tube? How many houses are you supposed to look at before making a choice, anyway?

Working with a good real estate agent can make all the difference. They can save you money and loads of time sifting through listings. They understand the neighbourhoods, can give you advice about school zones, and will point out home flaws you might not notice. Not all agents are created equal though. Considering that an agent could conceivably pocket up to $12,000 of your money on a $400,000 home if they're paid three percent in commission, it just makes sense to get the best agent money can buy.

To find an experienced, ethical agent, peruse the real estate listings, check websites, and ask for referrals. Don't forget to look for agents who specialize in the area you're interested in. For example, in Vancouver there are agents who specialize in downtown condos. Choose three to interview then give them a call. You'll want to be honest and let them know you're interviewing agents and see if you can meet for five or 10 minutes. Once you're face to face, ask relevant questions and listen to their answers. They should have some sort of general game plan mapped out for you. If you're not sure what to ask, use the "Get to know your agent" worksheet on the next page as a guide.

Before visiting any properties, the agent will help you decide what type of home you're looking for. A great agent will nail down more than a price and location, she'll find out what makes your family tick. Do you want to avoid a long commute? Are you looking for a home in a zone with good schools? How safe is the neighbourhood? Is it close to a busy intersection? Do you demand that all nearby streets have sidewalks so you can start a walking club? These are the things an experienced agent will address.

GET TO KNOW YOUR AGENT

Use this checklist to evaluate multiple agents before deciding who you would prefer to work with.

Worksheet No. 6

Name of Agent:	Contact:
Question	Answer
Which real estate company do you work for?	
How long have you been an agent?	
Do you have a licence?	
Do you hold any professional designations?	
Do you work with other agents or use assistants?	
What is the amount of commission that you charge?	
Which areas of the city/town do you work in or are the most familiar with?	
Do you understand what I am looking for in a home?	
Do you have experience working with first-time buyers? (only relevant if you are a first-time homebuyer)	
How many other buyers or sellers are you currently representing?	
Is there anything about you or your company that I haven't asked or that you think I should know?	
Can I have three references from other buyers you have worked with recently?	
Notes:	

Source: Canada Mortgage and Housing Corporation

ON THE PROWL

Consider the first trip out a learning experience for you and the agent. You will quickly get a sense of how closely she has been listening to your wants and needs. She will find out how serious you are about finding a home with a laundry room on the second floor. At this point you and the agent can determine what you really want, as opposed to what you thought you wanted.

Keep a poker face and stay quiet when you're looking at a home in which the sellers or their agent are hovering in the background. Negative comments insult the seller. But saying something along the lines of, "Oh my god! I love the kitchen!" could mean you'll be paying top dollar for every single backsplash tile come negotiation time.

INVESTIGATE AND RUMINATE

If you've found a property you're interested in, you'll want to do the homebuyer's equivalent of kicking the tires to see what falls apart. Hire a home inspector who has met the provincial or regional association's certification requirements. (Check with the Canadian Association of Home and Property Inspectors.) But don't use the selling agent's inspector. To avoid conflict of interest, ask your mortgagor who they would recommend.

Accompany your inspector while she examines the home so you will understand what she's referring to in the written report. She'll point out anything from missing roof tiles to cracks in the foundation. She won't tell you not to buy a house, but she will let you know if you're looking at a pristine dwelling or a money pit waiting to happen.

Even if everything checks out, take a step back and look at your home's "must have" list again. Maybe you really wanted a fireplace, but this otherwise perfect house lacks one. Can you install one? How much would that cost? Maybe it makes more sense to look at other houses until the perfect one pops up. Many people fall in love with "the wrong house" because they're entranced by the professional staging and landscaping, but ignore mediocre or inappropriate floor plans. (For example, if you like to throw big parties every December, you'll want a house with a large footprint so guests can spread out, rather than a skinny four-level townhouse.)

You know what you want. Stick with the plan.

CLOSING THE DEAL

Congratulations! You've finally found the property you want. Now the agent will help you decide on an offer—without going too high or too low—and will negotiate on your behalf. Depending on how hot the market is, count on staying close to the phone at this stage or even sitting outside in the car waiting for questions. You might be asked to raise your offer or nix some conditions you have. A less sought-after house will equal a more positive experience. In fact, you might be able to make even more demands if the seller is desperate.

After the closing, the lawyer takes over and drafts contracts you will have to sign. On moving day, you'll pick up the keys at the lawyer's office.

OTHER COSTS

Beyond down payments and interest, you'll also want to set aside money to pay for closing costs—up to 1.5 percent of the basic purchase price. A professional building inspector can run you $200 and up for a written report according to CMHC. (Tip: always get a professional to look over your home before you buy. Between finding cracks in the foundation, poor air circulation in the roof, and other problems you might not see, that $200 could save you thousands in repair bills, not to mention heartache and stress. The only time you might wind up signing the dotted line without one? You're buying in a super-hot sellers' market and an inspection will nix your chances of "winning" the house.) You will also be responsible for paying fees and disbursements for the lawyer or notary acting for you and paying the land transfer tax (a one time tax based on a percentage of the purchase price and/or the mortgage amount). And remember your property insurance. You have to have that in place by the closing date too.

As well, if you plan to change mortgage providers, investigate whether or not you'll have to pay a penalty for breaking the existing mortgage. Other incidental costs include rewiring, renovations, painting, and new furniture or artwork for the walls. Perhaps you're moving from a condo to a detached house and a new lawn mower and gardening tools are in the cards.

Little costs also add up: mail forwarding, change of address fees, and utilities.

Finally, the moving cost itself will range from almost free (think a borrowed van, a few friends, and a case of beer at the end of the day) to thousands of dollars if you choose a professional moving service and your new dwelling is far away.

PAY DOWN YOUR MORTGAGE FAST

You've picked up the keys, unpacked boxes, met your neighbours, and plowed out the driveway after the first snowfall of the season. Now the fireplace's glow beckons and you're ready to call it a night. Hold that thought, because there's still one more abode-related task you'll want to consider: overpaying your mortgage.

It sounds crazy, doesn't it? You would never choose to overpay for a restaurant meal, new pair of jeans, or airline ticket to the tropics, but when it comes to your mortgage, paying more than is necessary—at least in the short term—is the smartest financial move any of us can make. Here's why: on a $200,000 mortgage at six percent interest amortized over 25 years, you'll pay an extra $183,883 in interest. You're nearly doubling the cost of your home! That's after tax dollars too.

But there's a way to pay off your mortgage faster and save thousands in interest charges. Let's look at a few ways to accelerate your payments and make that mortgage history.

APPRAISE THIS!

If the U.S. mortgage catastrophe of 2008 and 2009 taught us nothing else, it's that buying more house than we can actually afford is one of the biggest real estate errors we're likely to make. (Who can forget those photos taken of American suburban streets lined with "For Sale" signs and abandoned million-dollar homes?)

Unfortunately, it's still easy to become house poor after being sucked into signing for a larger mortgage than you can pay. While many buyers wisely get pre-approved for a mortgage before they head out into the market, they often mistakenly believe that what the bank is willing to float them is actually what they can afford to pay. Others find themselves in serious financial trouble when interest rates start climbing again.

Remember that financial institutions are in the business of loaning money and making money on that loan by betting you can't pay it all back in, say, seven months. (Some loan documents even stipulate that you're not allowed to pay the money back too quickly.) So although the bank has calculated your GDS and may determine that you can afford to buy a $500,000 home, they're probably being a tad optimistic. For instance, they don't know that you plan on having two more children or that you expect to travel this year. They don't have a crystal ball to tell them that your car is about to bite the dust at the side of the highway and you'll have to spring for a new one. You are the only one who can make truly educated guesses about your future financial situation.

Living below your means—in other words, buying a home that costs less than what the bank will loan you—saves you a bundle of money and your nerves. ■

PREPAY TO SAVE

To make a big impact on the mortgage dollars you pay, particularly in the early days, prepay your mortgage, meaning put an extra payment against the mortgage. Some policies even allow you to "double up" your payments and put that money against the principal. When you do this at the beginning of your amortization period, you avoid compounding that money and save big. On a $100,000 mortgage at seven percent, one extra payment of $1,000 can eventually save you $4,100 in interest. Keep it going every year to save even more.

Finding the dough each year can be as simple as investing in an RRSP and using the tax refund, brown bagging lunch twice a week ($20 per week × 50 weeks = $1,000), or paying off a loan and swinging the money to the mortgage.

DO IT BIWEEKLY

If you can't seem to find an extra thousand dollars all at once, use an accelerated weekly or biweekly payment option and you'll end up making one extra monthly payment each year anyway. As with prepayment, more of the principal is repaid sooner, leaving you with less interest to pay over the long haul. Again, you'll save big.

Here's how it breaks down:

If you pay monthly, a $300,000 mortgage at six percent amortized over 25 years will cost you $275,825.91 in interest. If you use an accelerated biweekly option, however, that same $300,000 mortgage at six percent amortized over 25 years means shelling out $223,014.85 in interest instead—a savings of $52,811.06. And you'll be mortgage free four years earlier!

GET A BETTER RATE

If you've negotiated a better interest rate, pretend nothing has changed. That's right. Even though you no longer have to pay as much, make the same payments each month or biweekly anyway. An additional $115 every month can save $23,000 in interest on a five percent mortgage. You'll be throwing your "mortgage or bust" party seven years sooner too.

WATCH THOSE CHARGES

If you are on a special discounted or fixed-rate deal, fast-tracking your mortgage payments may mean having to pay a costly early redemption penalty. Making extra payments to chop your mortgage down faster is not a good idea in this situation.

Neither should you repay some of your mortgage if you have heavy credit card debts. Remember, a six percent mortgage loan is still far cheaper than most other loans. It makes little sense to repay a mortgage at six percent if you have credit card debts demanding 15 to 20 percent.

WHEN IT'S TIME TO SELL

Are you dreaming of moving to better digs? If your abode is feeling a tad too humble these days and it's time to sell, there's good news and bad news for you. The good news is you've already been through the home-buying process so finding real estate agents and dealing with lawyers is less intimidating. Now the bad news: selling a home can be more work since you're probably doing two things at once—buying a new home and selling your old one. Here's a short guide to help you sell for top dollar while avoiding typical pitfalls that home sellers face:

PAY THE COMMISSION

Finding a real estate agent to sell your house is much like finding one when you buy, except you're looking for someone who can guide you through the process and negotiate for the best price. Again, ask for references and a list of other houses they have sold, as well as the length of time these houses were on the market. And don't forget referrals. If you already used an agent when you bought your current home and liked her, picking up the phone and hiring her again is obviously a no-brainer.

When you sell your home, expect to hand over about five percent or more of your total sale price, depending on the agent and your needs. For example, if you're selling a remote family cottage that requires a motorboat to see it, you'll pay more commission to offset the hassle factor.

DO IT YOURSELF

Many people who want to save on the commission decide to sell privately. The DIY approach will probably cost less than a tenth of what you will pay if you hire an agent. Just remember that if the buyer has an agent, that person will still want a commission to help the sale along.

If you opt for selling your home yourself, you'll have to be very accessible to potential buyers by phone, pager, or online. You're also going to have to incur the costs of advertising and hiring an appraiser and a lawyer. Be prepared to check any emotional attachment you have to your home at the door. Ask a friend who is willing to be honest what you should change around the house before putting it on the market. Or hire a home stager.

KNOW YOUR WORTH

Sellers tend to overestimate what their homes are worth. Just because the house at the end of the street sold for a bundle, it doesn't mean yours will too. Consult up to three realtors for an opinion. They're well versed in all of the factors that will influence the market value of your home. If you're still not convinced of the price they give you, you can always get a second opinion. Just be prepared to pay for it if you go the independent appraiser route. To find an appraiser, visit the Appraisal Institute of Canada website and search its database (Component.aicanada.ca/e/findappraiser_find.cfm).

TIME IT RIGHT

Buying and selling homes concurrently can send anyone reaching for the aspirin bottle. Do you buy a new home first then hope your current digs will sell? Or do you put your house on the market first before finding a new place to live? You want to avoid giving up your existing home before moving into the new one; having to find a temporary place to live and store furniture and other effects, while waiting for the new house to become available, can be a nightmare. Not to mention expensive. At the same time, you want to avoid committing to a new house using the equity in your existing home, only to find that you can't sell. That's even worse.

The best-case scenario would be to have a high enough income to carry both mortgages (if it comes to it) and to have the funds to pay for the new house without dipping into the equity of the old one. In this case, you would buy your new house first and once it's under contract and the new mortgage is arranged, you would put your old house on the market, setting a closing date after the closing on the new house. That way, you can stay in your old house until all the painting and small or large renovation projects are completed at the new one.

If you don't have enough money to carry both houses, you may need to cash out some of the equity in your existing house. Talk to your financial advisor, real estate agent, or mortgage advisor about how to do this and weigh the pros and cons.

Remember that the person buying your home is probably dealing with the same "buy it first or sell it first?" conundrum too. Often you can negotiate closing dates so everyone has some breathing room.

SPRUCE UP THE HOUSE

Without question, home staging or restyling a home's decor to impress the buyers trooping through is critical to selling. It can also garner you a higher price. So how much money do you pour into the house you're leaving? According to one study conducted by Maritz Research for Royal LePage, 54 percent of Canadians believe that $2,000 or more is the magic number. Staging experts agree. Even a meager $1,000 can go a long way toward paint, throw pillows, and fresh flowers to brighten a drab interior.

But before slapping a coat of paint onto your front door or adding a bit more lighting to the basement, ask yourself if you're ready to start treating your home as a commodity to be sold. It requires detachment and impartiality. So if you're having second thoughts about taking a favourite family portrait off the wall for a few weeks, maybe you're not quite ready to post that "For Sale" sign.

Here are a few other house-staging tips:

CURB APPEAL

Before prospective buyers step into your house, there's a good chance they've driven by it first, or at least looked at photos of it online. Make a great first impression by putting flowers and greenery in planters, mowing the lawn, and stashing the trash. Stow the kids' bikes away too, but if you're living in a neighbourhood that draws in lots of young families, leave the tree swing up as a clue that children are welcome.

CLEAN UP

Showing off a clean house is hands down the best way to sell it. Hire a professional cleaning service once a week until the home is sold. Between visits, get rid of odours by opening the windows (even for 15 minutes a day in the winter), sweep and wash the floors, and wipe down sinks. Don't forget to clean rugs and upholstery.

DE-CLUTTER

A pile of papers here, a stack of mail there. It's much harder for a buyer to envision living in your home when it's filled with your personal effects and, well, mess. Take out and store a third of your furniture if you have to. Rent a storage locker and haul your extra items there, or take them to a local consignment shop or charity if they're no longer needed. You can also ask a relative to store the stuff in their garage. Avoid using yours since buyers will want to see it.

PAINT AND REPAIR

A paint job can give a slightly rundown-looking house a new sheen. Clean up the palette and make it bright and neutral. Warm white, blue-grey, and taupe are good choices, but a little boring, so don't be afraid of painting an accent wall in another colour or shade. Fix leaky faucets and mouldy grouting in the bathroom.

MODERNIZE

Our homes are never as up-to-date as we think they are. Ditch those dusty-rose-coloured bubble curtains and shams or rip up the powder blue carpet and replace it with a neutral colour. Rent some contemporary art from a local gallery and buy a throw for the sofa.

CLOSE THE ZOO

Not everyone will love your cat, dog, guinea pig, or pet lizard as much as your family does. (Some buyers are allergic or even phobic.) Pets can be distracting too. Take them out of your home, if possible, when buyers drop in.

KEEP IT NATURAL

Today's homebuyers are a savvy bunch and they've watched enough home design shows to know when a home has been staged to the hilt. So avoid going overboard with scented candles and a fresh pie in the oven. Many people are now turned off by stager's "tricks" and wonder what you're trying to hide.

KNOW THE TERMS

It's no secret that between appraisals, down payments, and mortgages, the real estate game is rife with words and terms used at no other time in life (that is, unless you routinely refer to sex as a "conditional offer"). So even if this is your second or third time making the open house rounds, refer to this home-buyers' glossary to keep it all straight.

AMORTIZATION PERIOD: The actual number of years it will take to pay back your mortgage loan.

ANNIVERSARY: Many mortgage products allow you to make payments against the principal on the anniversary of the mortgage.

APPRAISAL: The process of determining the lending value of a property. Remember that the lending value does not actually take into consideration the current market, which could shoot your home's price into the stratosphere if the timing is right, or cause it to plunge if you try to sell in a buyers' market.

APPRECIATION: An increase of a property's value due to changes in market conditions or other reasons.

BIWEEKLY PAYMENT MORTGAGE: A mortgage that requires payments to be made every two weeks (instead of monthly). This is a fabulous way to slash down your mortgage faster.

CAPPED RATE: An interest rate with a predetermined ceiling, usually associated with a variable-rate mortgage.

CLOSED MORTGAGE: Locks you into a specific payment schedule. A penalty usually applies if you repay the loan in full before the end of a closed term.

CLOSING COSTS: Expenses in addition to the purchase price of a property and that are payable on the closing date. Examples include legal fees, land transfer taxes, and disbursements. They can total several thousand dollars.

CLOSING DATE: The date on which the sale of a property becomes final and the buyer takes possession.

CMHC: Canada Mortgage and Housing Corporation, a Crown corporation that administers the National Housing Act for the federal government and encourages the improvement of housing and living conditions for Canadians. CMHC is one of two sources for high-ratio mortgage insurance.

CONDITIONAL OFFER: An offer subject to conditions such as loan approval.

CONDOMINIUM FEE: A fee paid by the condo owner that is allocated to pay building expenses.

CONVENTIONAL MORTGAGE: A loan issued for up to 75 percent of the property's appraised value or purchase price, whichever is less.

CO-OPERATIVE (CO-OP): The residents of this type of housing complex don't actually own the dwelling they live in; they own shares in the corporation.

DEED: A legal document, signed by both parties, that transfers ownership.

DEFAULT: Failure to abide by the terms of a mortgage; may result in legal action such as foreclosure.

DOWN PAYMENT: The buyer's cash payment toward the property; the difference between the purchase price and the mortgage loan.

EASEMENT: The right to use another's property for a specific purpose (e.g., a shared driveway).

EQUITY: The difference between your home's value and the money you owe against it.

ESCROW: Funds that are set aside and held in trust, usually for payment of taxes and insurance on real property.

GEMI: GE Capital Mortgage Insurance Company of Canada, a private mortgage insurance company; one of two sources of high-ratio mortgage insurance.

GROSS DEBT SERVICE RATIO (GDS): The percentage of a borrower's monthly income that goes to mortgage payments, utilities, taxes, and half of condo fees. The percentage is arrived at by dividing your monthly shelter costs (principal, interest, property taxes, heating, and half of your condo fees, for instance) by your gross monthly income, and multiplying by 100. Lenders use this yardstick to measure a borrower's ability to make mortgage payments. For example, most lenders require that your ratio be no more than 32 percent.

HIGH-RATIO MORTGAGE: A mortgage that exceeds 75 percent of the home's appraised value. (These mortgages must be insured for payment.)

HOME INSURANCE: Insurance to cover both your home and its contents in the event of fire, theft, vandalism, etc. (also referred to as property insurance). This is different from mortgage life insurance, which pays the outstanding balance of your mortgage in full if you die.

HOT MARKET: A market where housing sales are up and the sales price is likely to be significantly higher than the asking (listing) price.

INSPECTION: The process of having a qualified home inspector identify potential strengths and weaknesses in a property so that you may have a good idea of its functional condition.

INTEREST ADJUSTMENT: The amount of interest due between the date your mortgage starts and the date from which the first mortgage payment is calculated. Avoid it by arranging to make your first mortgage payment exactly one payment period after your closing date.

LAND TRANSFER TAX, DEED TAX, OR PROPERTY PURCHASE TAX: A fee paid to the municipal and/or provincial government for the transferring of property from seller to buyer.

LEGAL FEES AND DISBURSEMENTS: Some of the legal costs associated with the sale or purchase of a property. It's in your best interest to engage the services of a real estate lawyer (or a notary in Quebec).

LIEN: A claim for money owed by a property owner to a supplier or contractor.

LISTING AGREEMENT: A legal agreement between the listing broker and the seller that describes the property for sale and states the services to be provided and the terms of payment. A commission is generally paid to the broker upon closing.

LISTING PRICE: The price at which the house is listed; also known as the asking price.

LUMP-SUM PAYMENT: An extra payment that you make to reduce the amount of your mortgage. This is the same as prepaying, which you cannot do if you have a closed mortgage.

MATURITY DATE: The end of the term of a mortgage loan, at which time you can pay off the mortgage or renew it.

MORTGAGE: A loan that you take out in order to buy property. The collateral is the property itself.

MORTGAGE BROKER: A person or company that offers mortgage products from several financial institutions, but does not loan the money from their own coffer. Mortgage brokers usually charge a fee or receive a commission for their services.

MORTGAGEE: The lender.

MORTGAGE INSURANCE: Applies to high-ratio mortgages. It protects the lender against loss if the borrower is unable to repay the mortgage.

MORTGAGE LIFE INSURANCE: Pays off the mortgage if the borrower dies so that his or her heirs do not assume the debt. If you have ample life insurance you may not need this insurance.

MORTGAGE RATE: The percentage of interest that you pay on top of the loan principal.

MORTGAGOR: The borrower.

MOVING EXPENSES: The cost of hiring packers, movers, or a rental van.

OFFER TO PURCHASE: A legally binding agreement between you and the person who owns the house you want to buy. It includes your offering price, what you expect to be included with the house, and the financial conditions of the sale (your financing arrangements, the closing date, etc.).

OPEN MORTGAGE: Allows partial or full payment of the principal at any time, without penalty.

PORTABILITY: A mortgage option that enables borrowers to take their current mortgage with them to another property without penalty.

PRE-APPROVED MORTGAGE: Qualifies you for a mortgage amount before you start shopping.

PREPAYMENT PENALTY: Money charged for an early repayment of debt.

PREPAYMENTS: Voluntary payments in addition to regular mortgage payments.

PROPERTY SURVEY: A legal description of your property, its location, and its dimensions (usually required by your mortgage lender).

REFINANCING: Increasing the amount of your current mortgage (at a new interest rate). The term of the new mortgage must be equal to or greater than the term remaining on your current mortgage.

RENEWAL: Renegotiation of a new mortgage loan term at the end of a negotiated term period.

SALES TAXES: Taxes applied to the purchase cost of a property. Some properties are exempt from sales tax and some are not. For instance, residential resale properties are usually GST exempt, while new properties require GST, although some may qualify for a rebate.

SATISFACTION OF MORTGAGE: The document issued by the mortgagee when the mortgage loan is paid in full. Also called a "release of mortgage," or the "holy mackerel, I'm free!" document. (Not really, but it should be.)

SECOND MORTGAGE: Additional financing, which usually has a shorter term and a higher interest rate than the first mortgage.

SERVICE CHARGES: Extra costs incurred when hooking up hydro, gas, phone, etc. to a new address.

SOFT MARKET: A market where housing sales are down and the sales price is likely to be significantly lower than the asking (listing) price.

SURVEY: A document that shows the boundaries of the property and specifies encroachments, easements, and the placement of buildings on the property.

TERM: The period during which the conditions of the mortgage apply and after which must be renegotiated.

TITLE SEARCH: An examination of municipal records to determine the legal ownership of property, usually performed by a title company.

TOTAL DEBT SERVICE RATIO (TDS): The percentage of the buyer or owner's gross annual income required to pay mortgage, utilities, insurance, debts, and all other payments.

VARIABLE-RATE MORTGAGE: A mortgage with an interest rate that changes with the market.

VERIFICATION OF EMPLOYMENT: The lender will sometimes contact an applicant's employer to verify information provided in a mortgage application—your income structure, how long you've been employed, your position, etc.

ANOTHER
REASON TO SELL

Do you remember the survey discussed earlier in this chapter that showed us how many women are buying homes solo today? For some, they simply want to stop paying a landlord; others need to feel the dirt of their own gardens under their fingernails. Still, many women who buy their own homes do it out of necessity. They've become separated or divorced, and now, more than ever, want a place of their own.

In the next chapter we're going to go deep into, if not the bedrooms, at least the spending habits, of couples that stay together versus those who part ways. We'll also examine the sticky side of pre-nups, combining finances, and how to come out of divorce holding our heads high—and our credit rating intact. Keep reading.

Chapter 7
MONEY
MEETS
MARRIAGE

....

On the face of it, Amy and Jared have it all: The monster home in the suburbs. A wine cellar stocked to the rafters. Vacations to far flung locales each summer. Who wouldn't envy them?

But behind closed doors, Amy and Jared's relationship is falling apart only two years after their wedding. Amy, who grew up in a financially secure household, is a saver and an investor. She not only uses terms like "annuity" and "zero-based budgeting," she knows what they mean. Jared's idea of long-term planning? Deciding what to do next Saturday night.

Amazingly, their starkly different money personalities barely registered with each other before they tied the knot. Amy loved that Jared was so fun, vibrant, and exciting. And if he threw around a bit of money? Well, that was his business, not hers. For his part, Amy's steady, quiet personality made Jared feel happy and safe.

Combining their incomes changed everything. Now Amy and Jared fight about money nearly every week. Jared thinks Amy needs to lighten up and spend her cash; she makes enough of it working as a contract lawyer. Meanwhile, Amy's sure Jared is going to sink them into a stack of bills they'll never be able to afford.

After one particularly brutal argument, they decide they need to get some help and hire a financial planner who specializes in family finance dynamics. The decision saves their marriage.

"Our attitudes about money are so incredibly different, but having an impartial third person there to help us figure out why we feel the way we do makes a huge difference," says Amy.

When the couple begins talking about how they grew up, Jared reveals that his working-class background has an impact on how anxious he feels about having money. If it's in his wallet, he feels a compulsion to spend it—because who knows if he'll ever have money again? Meanwhile, Amy's grandfather, who had lived through the Great Depression as a child, taught her to save, save, and save some more. She feels real fear that her money will dry up.

With the planner's guidance, what could have turned into a marriage-ending crisis actually ends up bringing the couple together. The brilliant solution? Jared would pay all the bills and feed his thrill for spending money at the same time. Amy would set aside most of her money to build up the couple's savings. Now the couple's finances are back in shape and they're much happier.

"Now that we understand why each of us spends and saves, we are able to support each other. We feel like we know where our money is taking us—together," Amy says.

D O YOU FIND YOURSELF ARGUING WITH YOUR SPOUSE or partner over what he or she spends? Is your partner frustrated that you've forgotten what paper money looks like and routinely give the credit cards a workout? Or maybe your disagreements are of the more passive-aggressive variety. You spend a load on flashy items out of spite. In response he becomes tightfisted with his funds.

But even if your own story is slightly less extreme, and you bicker about the bills rather than waging all-out war—guess what? You're normal. Few couples, married or common-law, are on the exact same financial spreadsheet. And because we all have different approaches to spending and saving, money easily becomes a relationship flashpoint.

Sometimes the money chasm that divides us is alarmingly deep. In this chapter we're going to take a look at why money has a way of tearing couples apart, and we'll give you practical and effective ways to bridge the gap. These tools are not only going to get you paying the bills on time, they will actually mend parts of your relationship you never even knew were broken.

We're also going to show you ways to protect yourself financially before your wedding, during your marriage, and, yes, if you and your spouse ever call it quits. Fingers crossed, divorce papers won't ever come your way, but as any financially savvy woman knows, it pays to be prepared.

MONEY IS SOMETHING ELSE

So why exactly do otherwise compatible and loving couples find themselves arguing over assets? There are a few reasons. First, financial friction is often not so much about clashing money styles as it is about what is left unsaid. You *assumed* he would pay this month's bills. He *expected* you to want to spend your holiday bonus to pay down the mortgage. And don't forget, when it comes to relationships, money is never just money. It's tied up in how we view ourselves and how our parents raised us.

Here's the second reason: how you handle money together acts as a window into how other areas of your lives connect. And the problem is, sometimes we don't connect—or communicate—at all.

"You're not allowed to talk about politics, sex, or religion. Money is so taboo, it's not even on the list," says Amanda Mills, founder of Loose Change Inc. She says it's that inability to talk about money that can lead to heartbreak. So while few people would willingly open up about their bank accounts at a dinner party, some couples actually bring that discomfort into their relationship—with disastrous results. It's a case of "if we don't talk about it, it don't exist."

Still, the money taboo may finally be getting kicked off the list for another reason: in the tell-all age of Oprah, Suze Orman, and couples coming clean about $120,000 consumer debt on national TV, money just isn't nearly as hush-hush a subject anymore. Perhaps that's one of the reasons why, according to a 2009 Canadian survey, 14 percent of couples said they had severe disagreements about financial matters, way down from 25 percent claiming pecuniary discord in 2005.

Yet there's one more hurdle to get past even if couples are talking deep into the night about spending styles and mortgage payments: deep-seated fear, anger, and disappointment about the relationship itself. Because money is bound so tightly with power, control, prestige, and security, anger about money is sometimes a mask for more serious problems. If you feel bitter about having to trade a career for family, or if you feel neglected by a spouse who travels too much for work, money can become the weapon of choice.

So what's the solution? If money seems to be unravelling the fabric of your union, and you just can't seem to come together in any meaningful way on the topic, find a good counsellor and work through relationship dynamics and resentments. It's important to get to the actual root of your disharmony, rather than blaming the not-so-almighty dollar.

If marriage or a common-law relationship is in your future, start talking about money now. Knowing that he or she pays bills on time, or that there is a $17,000 student loan looming, will cut out surprises later.

Once you have your relationship issues taken care of and you're finally able to see, like Amy and Jared, where you're both coming from and why, it's time to work together and get on the same financial page. No screaming required.

What's your style? What is your partner's? The first step is to identify your personal money styles and what you're bringing into the relationship. Rather than setting your sights on income, include acts of service too, such as taking care of the kids each Friday so the other person can work an extra shift. Are you the Supply Queen, responsible for the family's spending, while your spouse, the Treasury Guard, saves and invests? Work with, rather than against, these attributes. No blame.

Get the facts straight. Once you know who is in charge of what, shed light on your current financial facts. Go back to the budget section in Chapter 3 to remind yourself how it's done. How much are you spending and on what? Are you saving for retirement or to meet long-term financial goals? Do purchases eat in to what you both value the most?

Start a financial plan. To meet financial goals head on, you've got to have a plan. There's no shortage of free financial planning resources and tools online or at the library, and you can visit Chatelaine.com for smart money tips and advice. Another option is to hire a certified financial planner who will sit down with you together, listen to what you want to do with your lives, and then draft a financial plan that will hopefully get you there in good time. (And don't forget meeting periodically for "financial tune-ups" too!) Again, couples with explosive money issues should consider sitting down with a marriage counsellor before hitting up a financial planner for advice.

Learning how to work together on your finances will give you amazing results. Think about it. When a couple earns, spends, and saves independently they're often heading off in different directions instead of running happily toward the same goals. It's hard to win the race when you're aiming for separate finish lines.

For instance, let's say you both know that someday you want to buy a cottage by the lake. You put aside $150 each month in a mutual fund. Meanwhile, your spouse, filled with an increasing sense of wanderlust, books a last-minute trip to Thailand for you both. In the end it takes much longer to build enough wealth to buy the cottage since only one person is saving.

There's nothing wrong with one half of a duo changing his or her mind about a financial goal (unless it's retirement savings, of course). But that's a conversation that needs to happen so you can develop a new road map. Maybe after coming back from Thailand you both decide you have the travel bug and want to explore new cultures rather than being tied down to a cottage. Or perhaps the trip makes you both long for a cabin in the woods.

Either way, when you work together on your finances you'll be reinforcing positive results and living the lives you want side by side.

TALK IT OUT!

You're mad because he can't part with his cash. He's fuming because you spend like it's Boxing Day, every day. Need some advice about how to deal with arguments, better understand your mate, and put your financial affairs in order?

Do this: Make a money date. Couples who routinely take time to look at their finances, pay bills, and evaluate debt are able to manage money all the better than couples who don't. Start by making weekly dates until the situation is under control, then move money date night to one day every month. If you're having a tough time getting started, commit to 30 minutes one evening or over breakfast when you aren't tired. Set the timer if you must.

Do this: Track your cash. Amy and Jared did this for one month on a notepad to see who was spending what. No shame, no blame—just observe and learn. The exercise not only helps couples work on a shared goal, but it eventually builds trust. (If you need a refresher on how to track spending, go back to page 46.)

Do this: Set a freedom limit for minor purchases. No one is advocating that you ask permission to spend seven bucks on hairspray. Decide on a cap, say, $50 or $100, and know that as long as what you buy is under the limit, springing for that DVD is your right.

Do this: Open a wish account. There's no better way to get excited about budgeting and saving than by choosing something you both want, opening a savings account, and loading it up with cash to pay for it. Even better, this system can stand between you and your credit card if a trip to Fiji suddenly beckons. Dip into the wish account funds rather than reaching for the credit card to remain debt-free. ■

WHY PROPOSE A PRE-NUP?

You've bought the dress, picked out the cake, and the RSVPs are flooding in. You've even discussed money with your fiancé and know where you both stand on debt management, bill paying, and spending habits. You're all set for marriage, or remarriage. Just one more thing to consider: a pre-nuptial agreement.

A what the what? Yes, your best friend signed one about six months before she walked down the aisle and so did your aunt before tying the knot for the, well, fourth time. If it makes sense for them, how about you?

Pre-nups, the controversial contracts hashed out before marriage, aren't just for wealthy lovebirds anymore. While they were once used to protect rich men from gold-digging women, perceptions about the pre-nup have changed. And now that women have more economic power, we are turning to these agreements to protect assets such as a house, an accumulated pension, or a business. We're looking for legal security to avoid some very nasty surprises if the marriage folds—nearly four out of 10 do in the country—especially those who are marrying later in life and have more to lose financially. People living in common-law arrangements can use a pre-nup-type document to help define their rights, even if they never actually marry.

(If you're already married and stay up late at night worrying about what would happen if your husband called it quits— even if you're perfectly happy together now—you haven't missed the boat. A marriage contract, also known as a post-marital agreement, does the trick too. Both of your signatures must be witnessed by at least one person and the agreement takes effect immediately.)

It's not that anyone plans for divorce before their wedding day, but it certainly isn't a bad move to think of a pre-nup as insurance. After all, you insure your house and belongings against fire and flood to be on the safe side, not because you want a blaze to break out in the basement or a tsunami to rage down your street. Unless you have the power to look into the future and be 100 percent certain your relationship will hold, taking precautions makes sense.

IT'S THE LAW

The law is slightly different in each province when it comes to divorce settlements, but as an example, in Ontario you list all assets and their value both on your wedding day and on the day you part ways. What you originally brought into the marriage, apart from the family home, is yours to keep. You have to share any increase in value of those assets with your ex though.

So let's say you opened a cupcake store a year before you wed and about three years into the marriage, cupcakes were suddenly sizzling hot. Everyone wanted to jump on the craze. The result? Your business went gangbusters—but you'll now owe hubby half of the increased value of your business. Meanwhile, if your husband's stockbroker picked some winners and inflated the value of his retirement fund, half of the increase is yours too.

In British Columbia, however, there's a chance you would have to split even the items you brought into the marriage as long as your family used them. Granted, a judge can modify the 50/50 split if one person racked up serious debt or the marriage lasted less than five years. (It's not exactly fair to be forced to split that much-loved Partridge Family album collection you've been adding to for 20 years, if the marriage lasted all of 75 days!) But without a pre-nup, you could find yourself in the position of sharing everything you have.

Imagine inheriting a beloved family cottage that your grandfather built on Vancouver Island—and watching it drop into an ex-spouse's hands. The family fallout would be enormous.

And don't think, "What's the point in signing a pre-nup? Judges routinely overturn them." That's not the case. If you both had independent legal advice and the pre-nup was signed well before the day you got married—so you can't say you were pressured into it the day before the wedding—and the pre-nup is not considered blatantly unfair, you're generally bound to it.

HOW TO ASK YOUR PARTNER FOR A (GULP) PRE-NUP:

1. Be prepared for your fiancé to feel put out or hurt that you want one. Think about how you would feel if he asked you first.

2. Admit your feelings about a pre-nup too. Simply demanding one is much different than saying, "This makes me feel uncomfortable too, but we should at least consider this—together." Keep the subject open to discussion, even if you feel quite firm about wanting a pre-nup.

3. Pick your moment. Don't throw the idea out there when he's just walked in from work or after an argument. Discuss the topic early. Don't wait until the week before the wedding.

4. However you treat the discussion, know it's a learning experience that gives you insight into your future relationship and how the two of you will hold up in tough situations. ∎

WHAT THEY COST

Pre-nups can be as complex or as simple as you want them to be. You can itemize every little teacup and ratchet set in the house, or you can write up a version of, "what's mine is mine and what's yours is yours, and whatever we get together we split." Costs vary, from $1,500 for a simple agreement, to a few thousand dollars for one on the more complicated side that includes a few back and forth conversations between lawyers.

Even so, pre-nups have another thing going for them: they offer swifter, cheaper resolutions to marriage breakups than typical divorce proceedings, which can easily cost many thousands of dollars, particularly if there is a business involved.

Just don't be tempted to reach for one of the DIY pre-nup kits found at business supply stores or online. With so many assets on the line, get a lawyer who can explain the consequences of any action you decide to take.

WEDDING
DAY LITE

Nobody wants to start a marriage in the red—so why pay big money for white taffeta? It's hardly the best way to eliminate money fights in the early years of not-quite marital bliss. Considering that the average wedding in Canada is running in the neighbourhood of $20,000 to $25,000, some couples are beginning to reconsider what they spend, particularly if they're the ones footing the bill.

Going the cheap and cheerful route often leads to the best weddings anyway, says Jolyn Saramaga, creative director and wedding planner for Nuance Occasions in Edmonton. If you don't have money to burn, there's little chance you'll have a lame cookie-cutter, credit card–busting wedding attended by 200 people, but remembered by few five years later.

"The wedding should really be a celebration of the couple. If you're spending money just to have the best of everything, that's not a wedding," she says.

Still, no one wants to *look* cheap. So how can you walk the fine line between lavish spending and penny-pinching practices? Here are a few options:

- The number-one way to slash wedding costs is to trim your guest list. Every time you invite one more person, the costs of catering, favours, rentals, and other fees increase. Instead, set down rules such as: only friends

I've talked to in the last five years are invited, or, no dates for single people. If someone is really going to be put out by their elimination from the list, by all means invite them. Weddings are supposed to be about support and love, not hurt feelings. But make them the exception, rather than the rule.

- Cut back at the bar. If you limit the choices, you'll slow down consumption and possibly pay less for the bartender. Stick to simple drinks like wine, beer, and a couple of wedding-themed cocktails.

- Rethink your wedding's time or day of the week. Instead of going the traditional Saturday dinner and dance route, throw a cocktail reception on a Friday evening with fancy finger foods. Brunch receptions are also romantic—and much cheaper.

- Trim back the decor and spend your money on things that guests will see as they walk through the door. The rest of the room can be scaled back. If the room is gorgeously ornate to begin with, you can cut down even further. You can also choose less expensive centrepiece options. During the holidays you can hit up end-of-season sales for spectacularly inexpensive Christmas tree ornaments and put them in inexpensive glass bowls from dollar stores for a fraction of the cost of fresh flowers.

- Ask friends and family for help. Is your university pal a virtuoso on the piano? Ask her to play you down the aisle. Do you have a well-spoken uncle who can act as the officiant? Maybe your crafty friend will lend a helping hand with ceremony decorations, or your type-A, bossy sister can be the wedding planner. People are often delighted to be part of the process.

- Nix the return envelopes and supply self-addressed stamped postcards instead. Or, go 3.0 and ask people to RSVP via email or even Evite.com. All you really need to know is the number of people who are coming so you know how many rubber chicken plates to order.

- Turn to eBay and Craigslist for discounted wedding favours, cake toppers, ring pillows, and even dresses. Just be sure you check ratings so you know you're dealing with a respected eBay seller.

COMBINING YOUR FINANCES . . . OR NOT

Now that you're married, you share a bed, kids, and a mortgage. But do you share a bank account? You've probably seen a lot of opinions and advice floating around about whether or not couples should combine their finances when they get married. Some say it's best to amalgamate earnings in a joint account. Others recommend keeping it all separate so both people feel they have say in where the money goes. (No doubt it's tough to give up control if you've been making all of your own financial decisions for the past 15 or 20 years.) Or maybe it's best to subscribe to the "Yours, Mine, Ours" banking philosophy in which couples keep separate accounts and a joint one too.

To share or not to share? Only you can decide how the two of you handle your money, but here are a few factors to consider:

JOINT ACCOUNTS

The upside: Many couples consider putting both of their names on a single bank account—a right of passage for any marriage. The joint account makes it easier to track money, and if there is a disparity between salaries, the person making less doesn't feel that they're scrimping and saving while the other is living the high life. Also, if one of you should die, joint accounts are easier to access.

The downside: Loss of autonomy. If you decided to keep your maiden name after marriage, chances are good that chucking away some financial freedom will make you squirm. Sharing a joint account can also evoke feelings of resentment when one partner is contributing more than the other, or if someone entered the marriage with a lot of debt.

And don't forget gifts. How are you expected to pull money out of the account to buy your honey an extravagant present without tipping him off?

SEPARATE ACCOUNTS

The upside: Maintaining separate accounts allows each of you to keep some money for doing what's important to you. Separate accounts are also a must if you have even a small home-based business. You'll want to keep finances separate to make bookkeeping easier.

The downside: If one half of the couple is notoriously bad at money management, there is no one watching if his or her account goes into free fall. Secret shopping and other forms of financial infidelity can go on for years and ultimately blindside the spouse and ruin their entire joint financial picture.

THE ONE-TWO APPROACH

The upside: If you want the best of both worlds, set up a joint account for bills and mortgage or for rent payments, while retaining separate chequing accounts. To make it work, sit down and figure out how much of your income goes to these expenses each month. That's easy if you both make roughly the same income. You simply contribute a similar dollar amount. But if one person makes significantly more money, contribute a percentage amount instead. Either way, both people deposit an agreed upon amount into the account.

The biggest advantage to this system is that you'll both retain your financial independence and the bills still get paid. You know just enough about what your husband or partner is doing with his money, without getting bogged down in the details.

The downside: There are more accounts to keep on top of and, depending on how you set up payments, determining who owes what each month can eat up your precious time and cash in the form of bank fees.

TALK IT OUT!

Why is out-earning our partners so complicated? Many women who pull in more income than their spouse or partner still admit to feeling (secretly) uncomfortable about it all. Earning more money can make us feel important and admirable, but if we're 100 percent honest with ourselves, there's often still that niggling little voice whispering, "This is not the way it's supposed to be."

It's time to quash the thought. When it comes to bringing home the bacon in a pair of killer heels, female top-earners are in good company. A Statistics Canada study reveals that more than a quarter of Canadian working wives earn more than their husbands. Meanwhile, a U.S. survey indicates the vast majority of men say they wouldn't mind if their wives brought home a bigger paycheque. Only 12 percent of their more Neanderthalesque brethren would take offence.

So go out and earn your keep—and while you're at it, earn his too. ■

DIVORCE: IN DEBT
DO YOU PART

"You can't be serious," says Nicole, arms folded and standing in her kitchen with its gleaming sinks and restaurant-quality stove. She'd just had it remodelled a few months before.

But Tony is dead serious. Nicole's husband of six years wants to separate and eventually get divorced. Not that Nicole is completely blindsided the night he comes home from a client dinner looking worried and claiming they, "need to talk." For years their relationship has limped along. Tony works 70-hour weeks and Nicole's resentment grows over lonely evenings and cancelled holidays.

So, in some ways, Nicole is relieved when Tony finally calls it quits. She'd been thinking about divorce for years, but felt intimidated at the idea of being completely financially independent. And then there's the cost of divorce.

Nicole is right to worry. Ending a marriage can be even more expensive than the wedding that started it all. The cost of splitting one household into two—think double the insurance, utility bills, and more—is alarming. But even before you get to that point, shelling out upwards of $500 an hour to pay for a top-notch family lawyer is enough to put almost anyone in the poorhouse.

No wonder plenty of women feel they're too broke to get a divorce and opt to stay in unhappy marriages for financial reasons. They've probably heard that divorced women fare much worse financially than their exes after a breakup.

In fact, according to the National Population Health Survey, 43 percent of Canadian women who have undergone a marital breakup (such as divorce or separation) have a substantial decrease in household income, while only 15 percent of separated or divorced men experience a financial decline. What's more, nearly 30 percent of recently divorced or separated men actually experience an *improvement* in the ranking of their adjusted household income. And women? Less than 10 percent see their standard of living go up.

HOARDER IN THE COURT

But let's get back to the divorce process.

Aside from divorces that involve high-end legal representation and forensic accountants digging through paper trails, how much do they typically cost? Once lawyers get involved, you can expect to pay $10,000 just to get a contested divorce to the beginning stages; however, it's not uncommon to hear about lengthy, complex splits that skyrocket to $250,000. Maybe she's hell-bent on keeping her foot in his business. Perhaps he wants her to sell the pricey scarves and bags she hoards in the closet so they can split the cash—and she won't budge.

Most divorces with a moderate amount of conflict will run soon to be ex-couples at least $15,000 to $20,000 per person.

There are other cheaper alternatives out there. Office supply shops and bookstores sell do-it-yourself divorce kits. People who don't want to be bothered learning the minutiae of divorce law can also use a service like Untie The Knot Divorce Service Inc. (Untietheknot.ca), whose owner, based in Nelson, B.C., will complete the necessary paperwork for a fee ranging from $225 to $375 (plus court filing costs and taxes in some provinces) depending on your province and whether you have children. Even with provincial filing and processing fees, some divorces can be wrapped up for under a few thousand dollars.

Still, the reality is that most couples on the brink of divorce want more guidance, especially when dealing with custody issues and shared assets. To bridge the gap, many partners— who have no interest in paying someone big bucks to turn them into enemies—are now using a third option: mediation. A divorce mediator is an independent third party who helps couples negotiate a separation agreement without relying too much on the use of expensive lawyers.

Mediators, with a background in law themselves, charge between $100 and $300 an hour, or about half what a lawyer will charge. And because both people use the same mediator, the charge is hacked away even further, costing only a quarter of what a couple would pay for two divorce lawyers working in a backlogged court system. Even so, mediation can still drag on for months if couples go head to head over splitting assets or negotiating alimony. You can find mediators through provincial association lists, on the Web and even by searching the Yellow Pages (look under "mediation services").

PREPARE FOR DIVORCE

If your marriage comes to an end, it pays to make sure your financial security doesn't also go up in smoke. So, is there any way to protect yourself financially if you think you might be served with divorce papers or you want to get the ball rolling yourself? Absolutely. While the best protection is a pre-nuptial agreement or marriage contract, it may be too late for that. Instead:

Meet with a lawyer. Hopefully you'll never need one, but meeting with a family lawyer before your divorce is a sure thing will help you get your head around what divorce entails. Find out what it might cost you. Ask lots of questions. Family lawyers have a bunch of tips to help protect your finances if the worst happens.

Get accounts in order. Are all of your family's financial accounts in your spouse's name? Establish your own credit history by opening your own account or signing up for a low-interest credit card with a small limit. Buy a few items and pay them off in full each month. It's also crucial to gather copies of all the important financial documents, including wills, tax returns from the past three years, mortgage refinancing papers, bank statements, pension statements, any separate financial papers and insurance policies. Pay stubs and employment information could come in handy later too. Keep it all in a safe (read: secret) place.

Know what you're worth. Use the papers you've uncovered and try to determine the value of your family's assets, including retirement accounts and pensions. If your house is filled with valuable antiques or other items, get them appraised and take photos of them. Better yet, wander around your house with a video camera. The images will prove an item exists and may jog your memory about others you forgot you had.

Pretend it has already happened. While you're still married and before you initiate a divorce, create a realistic monthly budget you would expect to need as a single-income household. Remember to include any bills your spouse usually pays such as car insurance or municipal house taxes. You may end up being on the hook for them later. This will give the court, or mediator, a better understanding of what you need to live on.

In (your) name only. If you'll be receiving an inheritance soon, don't put it in both of your names or use it to pay for property or property expenses. You could end up losing half of what Great Aunt Margaret left you. Keep your inheritance separate from the marital estate.

Keep debt down. If you're about to get a divorce, your disposable income is about to take a serious financial hit. This is not the time to make major purchases, plan home renovations, and sink yourself into debt. You'll want to keep your assets as liquid as possible. Start building an emergency fund if you don't already have one. It will be subject to the 50/50 split like everything else, but the backup money will help you feel you have some power over the process. Another option is to apply for a line of credit instead.

Provide for yourself. And don't count on alimony payments even if your salary is lower than you partner's. Instead, make sure you can pay your bills and have income coming in. That means looking for work if you're not employed and staying put if you are.

Be forewarned, these steps will not make you feel good, but if divorce happens, you'll be very glad you put your emotions on hold and got the job done early. Whenever a relationship ends, it's always sad and shocking even if you knew it was coming. Who wants to be digging around for old tax papers in that state of mind?

TALK IT OUT!

If you think your spouse is attempting to hide assets during divorce proceedings, what should you do? Take action—and dig around for clues.

- Ask yourself if there are any financial documents that are no longer coming to your house. For instance, maybe stock account information, bank statements, or cancelled cheques are now being diverted to a post office box or another office. Diversion usually happens over time so keep a list of what lands in the mailbox each month or quarter.

- Gather documents such as bank and brokerage statements, tax returns, and credit card and other loan statements. They will show the pattern of income and expenses if you ever need them.

- Be suspicious if the balance in the joint chequing account is gradually diminishing. This may show that funds are being diverted to another account. (Or, that he's saving up to send you and the kids on a vacation for some much-needed relaxation once the divorce goes through.) ■

TALK IT OUT!

As a woman, your bottom line is more likely to take a beating than your former husband's after a breakup. But proving yet again that money doesn't buy happiness, it turns out women still feel better post split than men. In fact men are almost twice as likely to become depressed after they sign divorce papers. At least, that's what a Statistics Canada study found out when it looked at the relationship between Canadian married or cohabiting couples and depression. After divorce, men were six times more likely than women to say they had experienced an episode of depression. Divorced or separated women were 3.5 times more likely to experience depression than women still in relationships. ■

LIVING THE COMMON-LAW LIFE

Not everyone decides to saunter down the aisle, exchange vows, and pen marriage certificates. And now that the whole "living in sin" concept barely registers to many Canadians, shacking up without springing for a ring appeals to a growing number of couples.

Data from the 2006 Census indicates that common-law relationships are on the rise with 16 percent of all families falling under the category. Two decades before, they rang in at only seven percent. And people in Quebec say, "I don't" more than anyone else with a stunning 29 percent of all families in La Belle Province claiming common-law status.

Maybe marriage is not exactly your cup of tea either. You have a committed relationship and who needs a piece of paper to prove it? That's a good point, but it's in your best interest to understand that common-law marriage is not considered the equivalent to a legal marriage and is treated differently if the relationship should fall apart. So how does a common-law "divorce" work? Here's what you need to know:

- Your relationship is over when you say it's over.

- What's yours is yours and what's his is his. The basic rule, whenever a common-law couple separates, is that each person keeps their belongings (maybe the house is in your name, or the car). You're also both responsible for your own debts. It's a smart move to keep receipts for every larger purchase you buy, or smaller ones if they mean something to you. Some provinces have different rules than others though, so visit your provincial government's website to find out where you stand.

- Assets in both of your names get split down the middle. You'll need to decide if one person will buy out the other person's share, or if you will sell the property and divide the profit. If you can't decide what to do, the court will normally order that the asset be sold.

- Child support and child custody are handled like those for divorced couples. Child support supports the child, so it makes no difference if you're legally married or not. Similarly, child custody is decided according to what is in the best interest of the child. Marital status is not the issue.

WITH THIS MONEY
I THEE WED

Whether you walk down the aisle flanked by topiary balls in a church, go the common-law route, or opt for a city hall celebration, getting married and staying married is not just about joining lives. It's also about merging debts, assets, and financial dreams.

Now that you've learned how to talk to your spouse about money, and know the ins and outs of protecting your finances, it's time to discuss other ways you can use money as a means of looking after your financial needs and those of your family. In the next chapter, we'll take a quick peek at some financial "extras" every woman needs to consider before she can call herself a supreme money queen. We're talking insurance, wills, kids' expenses, emergency funds, charitable giving, and how to organize all the financial paper piles that seem to accumulate at home. Here we go.

Chapter 8
EVERYTHING ELSE

· ·

It's 3 a.m. and Kumiko is in bed and wide awake while her husband sleeps beside her. This morning she took a home pregnancy test and—surprise—it came back positive. It has been a beautiful, memorable day full of intermingled feelings of excitement and apprehension.

And it's the apprehension keeping Kumiko up. After today's eventful news, it's finally dawning on her that her financial picture is about to change in many new and unfamiliar ways. Now she can't keep her thoughts from spinning away.

To begin with, Kumiko just started a new job last week as an executive assistant for a commercial mortgage firm, and she is worried about breaking the news of her impending maternity leave to the new boss. She's also wondering how her little family will get by on the 55 percent of her current salary that Employment Insurance (EI) provides for that first year of parental leave. Kumiko and her husband are already struggling to pay the mortgage on their four-bedroom, two-bath home.

She worries about finding ways to pay for new baby clothes and save for her child's university education (she knows there's something out there called an RESP, but has no idea what it means), and Kumiko thinks it's time she and her husband Brian re-evaluate their life insurance policies and even draft a will. But what will that cost?

"It's amazing how nuts I made myself that night worrying about everything. The next morning I called my mom and she calmed me down. 'It will all work out. It always does,' she told me," Kumiko says now, a few years later. "She was so right."

After sitting down with her husband a couple of evenings later, the two got organized and drafted a five-year plan. They researched ways to save money on baby items and started asking around for clothes, bouncy seats, strollers, and cribs. They stopped eating out three days a week and stashed that $120 they saved in an emergency fund. By the time the baby arrived, they already had $4,000 worth of financial breathing space just in case they needed it.

Kumiko and Brian made some tougher decisions too when they realized that if they sold their house and bought a slightly smaller one closer to Brian's workplace, they would save a bundle each year in mortgage and transportation costs. They also bought more life insurance and finalized their will. It was tough, but now Kumiko sleeps well at night—at least when her preschooler and newborn aren't waking her up.

FAMILY LIFE CAN BE WONDERFUL, FRUSTRATING, JOY-ful, and demanding. And as it did with Kumiko, it can rob us of sleep when we try merging it with money. That's no surprise. Earning, spending, and saving never happen in a bubble. In this chapter, we're going to show you how to deal with some of those financial "extras" that many of us are faced with throughout our lives. You're going to get the lowdown on maternity leave benefits, saving up for your kids' education, and preparing for the unexpected—with insurance, emergency funds, and wills—no matter what life stage you're at. We're also going to help you determine how to prepare for a job loss, and how to donate to charity when you have work and are in the black again. Finally, you're going to learn the best ways to keep all your records of these things straight.

Let's start with kids—and what they cost us from cradle to grad.

MAKING SENSE OF MAT LEAVE

Just talk to any of our American friends and faster than it takes to blurt out, "Six weeks! You only get six weeks of mat leave?" you'll realize what a fabulous maternity and parental leave program we enjoy in Canada. You probably already know that having the option to take a year off work to bounce, burp, and bathe our babies is a godsend for many mothers who couldn't imagine going through labour and delivery, only to don a skirt, grab a breast pump, and head back to the office a few weeks later.

But how does mat leave work, anyway? Between employer top-ups (nice) and long waits for that first EI cheque (not so nice), what exactly should you expect when you're expecting?

KNOW YOUR TERMS

Let's start with the difference between two concepts: leave and benefits.

Put simply, "leave" is the period of time parents can take away from their jobs without pay and still be guaranteed a job to come back to. The amount of time you can take off depends on the province or territory you live in as well as a whole host of eligibility requirements you must meet. For example, Albertans receive 15 weeks of maternity leave (just for mom) and 37 weeks of parental leave (to be taken by either parent). Those lucky enough to be living in Quebec, however, can be forgiven for acting smug. They receive 18 weeks of mat leave and 52 weeks of parental leave. (For more information about what each province supplies in terms of leave and benefits, check out Hrsdc.gc.ca.)

Meanwhile, "benefits" refers to the actual money moms and dads receive from Employment Insurance (EI) or from the Québec Parental Insurance Plan (QPIP) in Quebec.

Here's how to remember what's what: Leave gets you the time off. Benefits show you the money.

HOW MUCH DO I GET?

We'd love to say that you will be able to take 52 weeks off and have the same amount of money rolling in as you did while you were working. Unfortunately, that's not usually the case. Instead, when you have a baby, you file your claim for EI or QPIP benefits and eventually you'll receive a cheque or an automatic deposit of 55 percent of your average insured earnings up to a maximum payment of $447 per week. (So if you've been raking in big money—heck, even medium money—before starting a family, be prepared for a sizable drop in income.)

The maximum payment period for maternity benefits outside Quebec is 15 weeks, while parental benefits last up to 35 weeks. Maternity benefits, not surprisingly, are doled out only to biological moms. Parental benefits, however, are more flexible since they can be split between mothers and fathers or partners any way that works for them. It's a nice option if three months into mat leave you realize you'd rather go back to work and he'd rather take some time off for a bit of daddy-daughter time.

Just remember to track the amount of time you've worked to ensure you're actually eligible for EI. To qualify, you need to have worked for at least 600 hours in the last 52 weeks, or since the last time you made an EI claim. Although that's only about 15 weeks of full-time work, more than one mom who has gone back to work part-time only to get pregnant again has struggled to log enough hours before the next baby comes. So remember to do your math.

Quebecers looking for QPIP benefits have it easier. They only need to make $2,000 in insurable income during the reference period—normally 52 weeks—and pay their QPIP premiums. They can also choose between a basic plan and a special plan:

Basic plan

- Moms receive 70 percent of their earnings in maternity benefits for 18 weeks
- Parental benefits cover seven weeks at 70 percent, followed by 55 percent for 25 weeks

Special plan

- Moms receive 75 percent of their earnings in maternity benefits for 15 weeks
- Parental benefits cover 75 percent for 25 weeks
- Adoptive parents receive benefits worth 28 weeks at 75 percent

The basic plan is a good bet for families willing to live on less, but receive money for a longer time. The special plan works for adoptive families and for those who anticipate going back to work earlier. Both plans offer dads an extra paternity benefit equalling 70 percent of the father's earnings for five weeks (basic plan) or 75 percent of his earnings for three weeks (special plan).

HOW DO I APPLY?

To apply for EI benefits, visit a Service Canada Centre or apply online (at Servicecanada.gc.ca) the moment you stop working. Trust us on this. You don't want to hang around at home for those two weeks before the delivery date. Take action, then you can go back to puttering and nesting.

For QPIP benefits, apply on the QPIP website (Rqap.gouv.qc.ca) or call its customer service centre at 1-888-610-7727.

EMPLOYER TOP-UPS

Wouldn't it be fantastic if your boss walked up to your desk and handed you a wad of bills saying, "Here's a little something to tide you over until you come back from mat leave." Who wouldn't take the stash and waddle out the door?

In reality, some Canadian employers do offer a subsidy that helps pay the way for new parents on leave. You've probably heard it referred to as parental top-up payments. In other words, the employer tops up your EI or QPIP benefits so you don't have to take such a financial hit while off work.

Let's say you're employed by an organization such as the Royal Canadian Mounted Police in Ottawa, which pays parental leave top-ups to 93 percent for 52 weeks for moms, dads, and adoptive parents. That means you'll receive your EI cheque for up to 55 percent of your earnings and the other 38 percent will come from the good people who hired you. Not bad at all.

But time for a reality check. Just look at any "top employers" lists out there and you'll see that few companies foot the bill for the full 52 weeks. Most employers that offer a top-up payment tend to be less generous, shelling out 75, 85, or 100 percent top-ups for, say, 12, 16, or 18 weeks. After that, you're back to making ends meet on EI.

There's one more rather important point. Be honest with yourself before agreeing to take a top-up payment, because if you decide to quit your job to stay home with the baby, you'll have to pay the top-up back. Some career experts advise that you postpone accepting employer top-ups until a few months into your mat leave. That way you'll have a better idea whether you'll want to go back to work or if your heart belongs at home.

BUT WHAT HAPPENS IF I'M ADOPTING?

As long as you meet EI or QPIP requirements, you are entitled to some benefits too. While maternity benefits are paid exclusively to biological mothers, adoptive mothers and fathers still receive parental benefits. Adoptive parents in Quebec, however, receive a special adoption benefit of 75 percent of earnings for 28 weeks. In addition, more progressive companies offer top-up payments for adoptive parents. Some, such as KPMG, the international accounting and consultancy firm, even foot the bill—or at least part of it—for the adoption costs.

WHAT IF I'M SELF-EMPLOYED?

We hate to break this to you, but as it stands right now, the self-employed in the country get diddly in terms of leave and benefits from the government, unless you live in—you guessed it—Quebec. (It's not a free ride though. Quebecers pay into QPIP through their tax premiums—and they must stop working during mat leave or at least reduce the time spent on the business by at least 40 percent.)

Some women find a way to get around this by having someone else—spouses, parents, or friends—incorporate the business and employ them. Not surprisingly, between giving up power—even if it is all in the head—and red tape related to EI payments and CPP required for incorporation, many self-employed women don't go the corporate route. So is there another option?

Enter the DIY maternity leave. Put simply, you save up and set aside money for the number of months you want to take off when the baby arrives. The downside is you have to plan for an event that is a bit of a moving target *and* set aside money each month that you probably would like to use now. The upside is that this DIY approach gives you ultimate flexibility. You figure out how long you want to be on leave, decide how much money you'll need to make that happen, and then start socking away the correlating cash.

Here's an example of how the DIY plan works:

Marie is a recently married 29-year-old self-employed graphic designer. She and her husband Steven know they want to have kids in a few years, so they sit down at the computer to make some plans.

Right now Marie is making an average of $3,200 each month after taxes. It's a good living and after paying a portion of their rent, whittling down student loans and car payments, and paying a few bills, Marie usually still has money at the end of the month. Since her student loan will be paid off within two years, Marie knows they could easily live on her husband's salary and $2,000 of her mat leave money each month if she reins in her purse-a-month habit.

Being self-employed, Marie worries about taking off a whole year to take care of her baby full time, but she definitely wants to be the main caregiver for those first six months. To pull that off, she will need to save $12,000 if she wants to take her mat leave in three years.

That means Marie and Steven must save $4,000 per year until their baby is born. Using an online bank calculator that tabulates how much money they'll need to save in a high-interest savings account each month, Marie and Steven get the number they're after: $336 per month, as long as their savings account continues to pay out 1.35 percent in interest.

It's not a perfect plan. (Is any plan ever perfect?) On one hand, Marie doesn't predict being put on bedrest for the last two months of her pregnancy, which would force her to slash her hours. She also doesn't realize that designer baby diaper bags are actually really, really pretty and that she'll be more than tempted to buy a few. On the other hand, for the first years of their baby's life the couple's entertainment and travel budgets drop naturally.

Still, having a savings plan in place means Marie enjoys the best of both worlds: control over her own working life and a way to take maternity leave.

BANK ON IT!

Tempted to make a little cash on the side while on maternity leave? Not so fast. If you work while receiving maternity benefits, your earnings will be deducted, dollar for dollar, from your EI cheque. If you work while on parental benefits, however, you can earn between $50 per week or up to 25 percent of your benefits—and in some areas of the country, more.

- Break out the travel guidebooks. Even while on leave, you're entitled to be paid for annual vacation time in most jurisdictions across Canada.

- If your newborn or newly adopted child is hospitalized, you can choose to claim parental benefits immediately following the child's birth or placement, or when she comes home from the hospital. For each week your child is hospitalized, the period during which you can claim parental benefits is extended, up to a maximum of 104 weeks.

- All benefits are taxable. Figures. But at least there's a chance you'll have dropped a tax bracket while you're on leave. ■

KIDS DON'T COME CHEAP

. . . but they can come cheap*er* if you follow a bit of advice from frugal parents in the know. Think about this:

- Your bundle of joy doesn't have to cost you a bundle of cash right after birth (that comes later with hockey equipment and designer clothes). Ask friends with kids older than yours for hand-me-down sleepers, onesies, and anything else they have on hand. Friends can't wait to get the growing piles of too-small clothes out of their homes. In fact, you'll probably end up with too much! Unless your buddy wants her clothes back, feel free to sell the extra to consignment stores and use your earnings to pay for diapers.

- Your house is the single biggest expense when raising children, eating up at least 32 percent of your pay. One way to keep that cost down is to stay put. While it's estimated that every new child warrants 100 to 150 extra square feet, you don't have to move to bigger digs or launch major renovation projects. Your kids will be perfectly fine if you stick two of them in one bedroom. (They may actually grow closer as a result.) And if the idea of one bathroom for three teens gives you night sweats, consider installing a small powder room under the stairs instead of spending upwards of $15,000 for a new full bathroom. Because when you think about it, all they really need is an extra mirror and a door that locks.

- Another option is moving to a less pricey location (just do this when the kids are little if you can). Kira and Dave Carpenter ditched their mid-town Toronto neighbourhood when a two-bedroom bungalow on their street went for $500,000. They bought a three-bedroom home with a huge loft for $270,000 in downtown Guelph, about an hour away, and now work from home at least part of the time. What's more, they cut their $1,500 per month daycare bill in half after the move.

- Set strict limits with your kids—and stick to them. It's easy to hand money to older children when they're running out the door with their friends. But next time they ask for a twenty, think about what you're doing. Call a family meeting and tell everyone it's time to budget. For example, tell your kids they'll get $7 a week for fast food. Or enough for one night out at the movies. Or $300 per season for clothes. If they want more money and don't have a job already, let them know they're welcome to find one and pay for any extra expenses out of their own wages.

- Instead of buying new toys for younger kids, swap them out instead. Set up toy swap dates with parents of kids similar in age to yours and orchestrate some trades. The toys feel new, but they're free. (Just set ground rules about what to do when a child breaks a borrowed toy. Perhaps toys only under a certain dollar limit can be traded. Or only toys the child doesn't really care about.)

These are just a few ideas to get you thinking about ways to cut costs when you have kids. For more inspired ideas, visit Chatelaine.com forums, where you can also pass along your own great money-saving strategies.

RESP(ECT) YOUR KIDS' EDUCATION

Have you looked into the cost of post-secondary education lately? For a little illumination bound to induce heart palpitations, visit the university cost calculator at Canadianbuisness. com. Just pick a province, university, and faculty you think your darling scholar will eventually end up in, click a few more buttons and, voila, you're staring at the cold, hard total cost. Other post-secondary options—community and technical colleges—don't come cheap either, with some tuition fees running upwards of $4,000 a year for full-time studies.

It isn't pretty. Take a four-year arts degree from Queen's University in Kingston, Ont., for example. Factor in tuition, all of the extra athletic and student association fees, plus a room and meal plan, and you will be forking over $43,814 by graduation day. Not every student will live on campus all four years, and this tab doesn't include transportation, entertainment costs, or even textbooks, but the numbers do give new parents a sense of what financial maelstrom may be on the horizon.

And, with inflation and budget cutbacks nudging the fees higher and higher, who knows what you'll be paying in 18 years?

If you think saving up that kind of money will keep you broke until junior leaves home, you're going to be happily surprised. By saving a few dollars a day, you'll have plenty of money to make learning a priority.

Enter the Registered Education Savings Plan, or RESP, one of the most popular plans parents can use to save money for their kids' university or college while collecting free money from the government. That's right: free.

So how does an RESP work—and how can you make it work for you?

THE BASICS

You can contribute as much as you want each year, which grows tax-free until it's withdrawn, up to a lifetime limit of $50,000 per child. Unlike an RRSP, your contributions will not lower your taxes today, but because your child actually withdraws the money in the future, between tax breaks for tuition and the fact that he or she probably won't be working full-time while in school, your child will be paying much lower taxes on the funds. Here's the best part: for every $2,500 you throw at the RESP, the government chips in an extra $500 in Canada Education Savings Grant (CESG) funds. In other words, the

CESG will match up to 20 percent of contributions to the $500 maximum. The CESG lifetime limit is $7,200.

If you miss a year, you can double your contributions the next year and receive the grant (although you miss out on the benefits of compounding interest.)

WHAT YOU'LL SAVE

As we mentioned before, you can save for your child's education without bankrupting yourself in the process. Here's how: save a little bit every month, maybe that $100 child tax benefit, and as long as your investment makes a respectable return (you can consider six percent as a relatively conservative estimate over the long term) you'll wind up with what you need.

As an example, let's assume you decide to start an RESP for your five-year-old. You didn't get around to saving right from birth, but that's okay. You've had a lot on your plate. So you visit your bank's website, take a look at what RESP options it offers, and you decide on a mutual fund. You take your RRSP tax refund and invest $2,000 in the RESP to start. Then, every year you plunk $2,000 into that RESP at the beginning of the year using holiday bonus money. (You can also make monthly contributions automatically, which will run you $166.67— and that's a great solution for anyone who doesn't come into a big lump sum once each year. It just won't compound quite as quickly.) Meanwhile, the government kicks in $500 extra dollars annually.

So what does your $5.48 per day earn you after 13 years of saving? According to RESP calculators at Canadian Business Online, a cool $50,000 pre-taxes. Check out the RESP education savings calculator at Canadianbusiness.com and run some of your own numbers to see what you can make with just dollars a day.

FAMILY OR INDIVIDUAL

You'll want to figure out if you are going to open an individual or family RESP. If you have more than one child, the family option allows you to share benefits amongst siblings. That means that although contribution and CESG limits apply to each child within the plan, if your independent son decides to use his summer job money to pay tuition for the last two years and doesn't use his full share of the money (we can always dream, right?) your daughter can use it later for her law degree.

Anyone can open an individual RESP for one child, but only immediate family members can contribute to a family plan.

WHAT TO INVEST IN

You have more options than ever when it comes to choosing an RESP investment, but they'll always fall into one of two basic camps: scholarship plans—also known as pooled plans—and non-scholarship RESPs, which some people refer to as self-directed plans.

Group plans have been around since the 1960s in Canada and at one time they were the only game in town. They've recently fallen out of favour, however, due to their inflexibility (many only allow payouts once each school year instead of whenever a student needs the money) and costly up-front enrollment, administrative, trustee, and depository fees. Money is "pooled" together from everyone who buys in, and is usually put in to ultra-conservative investments. While this method seems safe, you have to play by the rules, or risk losing a lot of money.

For instance, if your child decides to join a band and tour Japan when he hits 18 instead of going to school, you may forfeit the interest on your contributions for that child. Meanwhile, the other students still in the pool who continue their studies divvy up all of the money—including *your* interest—amongst themselves. That's great for them, but not at all good for you.

In other cases, investors who find themselves short of cash one year and can't make a contribution could find themselves kicked out of the pool entirely. It's for reasons like these that the plans have drawn serious criticism from regulators for dubious marketing tactics.

Self-directed plans, in contrast, have a lot going for them. They're available from almost any financial institution and have the same investment range as RRSPs. You get to decide exactly where you want your money invested, whether that's GICs, mutual funds, or stocks. Canadian and international investments both make the cut.

The downside is that you'll have to keep a closer watch on how the investments are doing since your investment time horizon is shorter, about 18 years. In the first few years though, most people can afford to be a bit more aggressive with their investment style. The upside is your returns could be much higher with a self-directed plan. But, when you think about it, even if you only earn two or three percent, the CESG automatically gives you a 20 percent boost on the first $2,500. Not many investments can boast a number like *that*. Investors who want a medium amount of risk would benefit from a well-diversified mutual fund or even an index fund.

Here's one more reason to choose a self-directed plan: flexibility. You can take all the money out in the first year of your child's post-secondary schooling, or even wait until grad school—just as long as you close the plan within the prescribed 35-year limit.

And if your daughter decides against university or college or you no longer have money to contribute, all is not lost. You keep your contributions, and the income earned on the money is lost only if your RESP contract says it is. You will, however, lose your CESG government contributions.

Here are a few more RESP tips:

- Contribute as early in the calendar year as possible so your money can gain the full year's worth of tax sheltered compound growth.

- If you can, contribute as much as possible for the first three years. Yes, this is going to be tough if you're already paying for daycare and diapers, but do whatever you can to front-load your contributions now to take advantage of compound interest. You'll still get the full CESG amount too.

- When you're only a few years away from high school graduation day, it's time to re-evaluate your RESP portfolio and rebalance it so it has a more conservative asset allocation. The last thing you want is to lose a chunk of money six months before heading off to university. Of course if the market is already down, you might want to hold tight and hope there's an upturn coming soon.

- You can withdraw the interest as taxable income and pay an additional 20 percent penalty tax. In this case, your principal will be returned to you tax-free and the CESG will be returned to the government.

- Remember, you don't have to shoulder the financial burden for you children's education alone. Many parents rightly expect their kids to contribute to their own education too. Not only will you be teaching your kids how to save for larger goals, but they'll appreciate their education much more if the experience isn't handed to them on a school crest–encrusted silver platter. Some parents expect their teens to contribute $2,000 or $3,000 per year of school, while others offer to pay for all school expenses for year one and year four. If the kids pay their way for years two and three, that free ride in their last year of school is something to work for. Do what's right for you.

PICK YOUR INSURANCE WELL

Quick! How much life, home, auto, disability, or health insurance do you have? If you're not sure, you're a lot like many people who blithely sign jargon-filled, head-spinning benefits packages at work, or when they buy a car or home, without a second thought. Who can blame them? Reading insurance policies can be an exercise in confused, blurry-eyed boredom.

But, particularly when it comes to life insurance, it's incredibly important that you push through this tedium and get what you need for one simple, but very important reason: you contribute, financially and emotionally, to your family's well-being.

You need life insurance for the same reason your spouse or partner does: to protect the family, replace lost income, and pay off debt obligations. Because the majority of Canadian women now work outside the home, their deaths would result in slashing their families' much-needed income.

If you are a stay-at-home mom, you contribute hugely as well. Think about it. You keep the kids fed, clothed, diapered, and entertained. You provide dinner on the table and clean clothes folded and put away. You sign school permission forms and make sure bills are paid. You might not bring home the bacon, unless it's from the market, but the services you contribute to your family are invaluable. If you were to die or become debilitated in some way, your partner would either be forced to scale back his work hours, take grief leave or hire someone to take over all of the tasks you once performed. Either way, the family's standard of living would plummet.

Even single women without dependants would benefit from having some life or critical illness insurance. As macabre as it is to think about, life insurance would help pay for any of your funeral, cremation, or burial costs. Without insurance, or an employer's death benefit, your parents, or other people close to you, could end up footing the bill. A $7,600 invoice—the average cost of funeral expenses in Canada—is hardly the kind of financial burden you would want to leave behind. Yes, you might be eligible for the Canada Pension Plan death benefit, a one-time, lump-sum payment made to a deceased contributor's estate, but it only pays for a very basic funeral and burial.

And in the case of critical illness insurance, if you were to be diagnosed with, say, uterine or breast cancer that required rounds of chemo, you would be able to take the lump sum and use it to pay rent and bills while taking time off work to recover. The money would also come in handy for private nursing services if you needed extra care some days. This kind of insurance is particularly important for the self-employed who don't receive this kind of benefit from their employer.

Considering all of these significant reasons to carry adequate insurance policies, why do women—as many as 40 percent according to some industry estimates—have no life insurance at all? Even more astounding is that of those who are listed as an insured party, coverage for women accounts for a mere fraction of their policy's total dollar value. In most cases, the man's life is worth the lion's share—even if his wife contributes just as much to the family's bottom line.

Other than wanting to avoid thinking about death or other calamities, many people shun the topic because they worry they can't afford insurance. But you might be surprised by what's available. Say you are 45 and in good health. A 15-year policy for $100,000 could cost you about $250 a year in premiums. Younger women would pay even less. And more good news? Simply being female works in your favour when it comes to all kinds of insurance since women tend to live longer and are known for being safer, more responsible drivers. You're a lower insurance risk.

So, between health, life, auto, disability, and home insurance, how do you pick what you need and figure out how much coverage to buy?

HEALTH

The good news first: most Canadian residents are covered through provincial health care and benefits from work, which is usually all the coverage they will ever need. But these policies don't always cover the full cost of supplementary services such as chiropractic care, massage therapy, holistic services, wheelchairs, eye exams, crutches, or full orthodontic care for the kids. It's not a bad idea to build a quasi-emergency fund for these types of expenses.

You might also want to take out additional health insurance if you're leaving Canada to travel, particularly to the U.S. where medical care can bankrupt you without it. These travel-insurance policies are an excellent deal too. An average plan will set you back a mere $2 to $7 a day for a trip to the States. But, as with all types of insurance, read the fine print and know what you're buying.

LIFE

There are three major types of life insurance policies you can choose from: term, whole life, and universal. Most financial advisors suggest the more budget-friendly term insurance, which is only good for a specified amount of time—say, 10 or 15 years. It's useful for covering temporary needs, such as your mortgage if you die before it is paid off. The insurance is there to save your spouse from foreclosure or a forced sale if he can no longer afford the payments without your income.

Insurance agents will often suggest that you sign up for between five and seven times your current net income—so if you make $45,000 a year, buy at least $225,000 worth of insurance. But you also need to consider what stage you are at in your life, since your insurance needs will change as your family or employment situations change. Single women will want to be able to cover last debts and end-of-life expenses. Moms will want to be able to also cover their children's food, clothing, shelter, and even post-secondary education.

Or run these numbers: Determine what your short-term needs would be, add the figure to long-term expenses and minus the total from all sources of income you hope to have coming in. This combined total represents the minimum life insurance you would need.

And while you're at it, think about picking up some critical illness insurance too. These policies, which vary in cost depending on your age and medical conditions, pay out a lump sum for expenses not covered by health insurance if you become seriously ill (think cancer, stroke, or a heart attack). Critical illness insurance would pay for things like a hotel room close to the hospital for family members, rent or mortgage payments until you're feeling better again, or a caregiver for the kids. Some agents call it the most necessary but underutilized form of insurance—but again, read the fine print and find out exactly what illnesses it pays out for.

HOME

Standard home insurance policies typically cover fire, theft, and vandalism, but some policies exclude damage caused by pets and certain types of flooding. You'll also want to remember that home insurance will typically reimburse you for only a set fraction of what you paid for your belongings. Books and business computers have firm maximum limits, for example. A more expensive policy will extend your coverage on other goods to 100 percent.

Give new meaning to "your home away from home." If you have a child going to school in another city, or an elderly parent in a health-care facility, your policy may cover their possessions as well.

If you do have to make a claim, you can make the process quicker and easier by keeping a home inventory by using digital photos or video to keep a record of your stuff. Then put it on a disc and store it somewhere other than in your house. The Insurance Bureau of Canada has free software to help create a home inventory, available at Ibc.ca.

But what about renters? Tenants are often under the false impression that their landlord's policy covers them too. Not always. If a tenant is negligent and causes the damage, the owner's insurance company may even have the right to take the tenant to court to recover what they paid out. So if you're a renter, it might make sense to purchase policies that cover liability, personal belongings, and even additional living expenses if you need to move out while your home is being repaired.

AUTOMOBILE

By law, all drivers need car insurance before they can drive their vehicle off the lot, but take some time to shop around for the best rates. Before they decide on your premium, insurance companies consider everything from the number of drivers, to how many kilometres you'll drive, to the car's make and model.

If you already have home insurance, you may be able to get a better deal in some provinces if you buy auto insurance from the same company. Either way, car insurers offer lots of coverage options. Beyond the basic package, you can sign up for features such as accident forgiveness. Just don't "forget" to tell your insurance company if you make any modifications to your car, add or remove any drivers from the policy, or if your teen passes her driver's test and is ready to hit the road.

And never make a false claim. Not only is insurance fraud a crime, but insurance companies are dogged about catching fraudsters in action—fraudsters who are costing them more than $3 billion each year, according to the Insurance Bureau of Canada. Trust us, they want their money back.

DISABILITY

We all think that we're invincible and that no great harm will ever come to us. Wrong. At least at some point in our lives, we could get hurt, experience mental illness, or contract a disease and no longer be able to do our jobs. If you have a group insurance plan, your employer is likely paying for your disability insurance, which can cost them only a few dollars per employee per month if they work in an office. If they aren't buying it for you, consider buying it yourself.

But—we'll say this one final time—read the fine print. You might think being flat on your back after an injury qualifies as a disability, but you could find out your insurance company doesn't agree. You can still call clients from bed, right?

BANK ON IT!

Are you thinking about ditching your old car and driving off the lot with a new one? Before deciding on the make and model, take a moment to think about how the choices you make will affect the price of your auto insurance.

Pay up. Generally, the more expensive the car, the more you'll pay in premiums each month.

Pay down. Some insurance companies will give you a better rate if you select a four-door vehicle over one with two doors.

Pay up. Due to higher rates of vandalism, collisions, and theft, you'll pay more for your car if you live in an urban centre.

Pay down. Installing anti-theft devices will often drive down your insurance rates.

Pay up. Drivers who use their cars for an hour-long slog between home and work each day rack up stress on the road—and higher premiums.

Pay down. Consider joining a carpool, hopping on public transit, or taking the commuter train to work a few days a week. By reducing your driving mileage, your premiums may come down.

Pay up. Fender benders won't endear you to the people who calculate your insurance rates. Drivers who cause collisions generally pay more than those who are accident-free.

Pay down. If you're a long-time driver, it never hurts to take a quick weekend refresher class with a driving school to become a safe-driving queen and keep your record clean and your rates as low as possible. Despite its name, Young Drivers of Canada runs some excellent classroom courses that go over all those safe driving tips you've forgotten about—or were never taught in the first place. ■

SAVE FOR AN EMERGENCY

If there's one thing you need to remember about saving up for a rainy day it's that someday, at some time, it's going to pour buckets. That's just life. So it's easy to understand why an emergency fund is so important to keeping you financially afloat even when water is flooding in.

An emergency fund—most experts agree that you should have between three and six months' worth of living expenses put aside—helps you prepare for life's emergencies such as losing your job, losing your home and possessions in a fire (insurance only pays for a portion of your items' value, so you have to cover the rest), or if you become ill and can't work for a while.

If three or six months sounds daunting, just remember that you're not saving the equivalent of your *earnings* for those months, just your *expenses*. And there's a good chance you'll be able to scale way back on what you pay out during the time you're off searching for work or hobbling around on crutches. If you're still scared of the figure, be aware that some financial planners suggest simply setting up a comparable line of credit and focussing on paying down debt and building an RRSP.

In any case, the key, when it comes to adding to an emergency fund, is to start small. Yes, accumulating $12,000 or $20,000 will take some time, but if you make your immediate savings goals small and manageable, you're more likely going to stick with it for the long haul. So approach your bank, credit union, or online bank such as ING DIRECT, and open a savings account. Then get in the habit of making regular deposits weekly, biweekly, or monthly. Once you feel you can start adding more, up your contributions.

Remember it's important to keep this money as liquid as possible. So no stocks, bonds, or mutual funds. Keep it in a money market or high-interest savings account. The name of the game is keeping this cash safe.

BEATING TEMPTATION

You have $15,000 sitting in your savings account ready for any crisis. So why do you suddenly feel the urge to spend it? Here's the issue: even though our brains tell us we'll need the money someday when the worst happens, our hearts just won't believe it. A crisis? Other people have those.

The other problem is that the definition of "an emergency" is different for everyone and for some, nearly anything qualifies. That surprise car maintenance? Emergency. A new furnace? Emergency. Winter too long and too cold? That's an emergency for sure, right? Better use the funds for a vacation in Key West. Obviously, that's not what an emergency fund is for.

Here are a few things to remember to keep your eye on the prize:

- Sure, you want to keep your emergency fund in a liquid state, but it shouldn't be so easy to access that you're tempted to dip in whenever. Keep your fund far away from your chequing account and never link it to your ATM card or chequebook. If you need your money, you're going to have to call someone or show up at the bank.

- Only touch the money if, by not doing so, you'll be putting yourself in dire financial straits.

- It's okay to have more than one emergency fund. In fact, opening more than one account is the perfect solution for a lot of people who want to be prepared for anything. Aside from a main emergency fund, open separate accounts for house repairs, car repairs, and holiday and gift expenses. These situations, while not quite emergencies, come up all the time.

Particularly if you lose your job or are hit by a catastrophe, you'll be ready for it and you'll come out on the other side with your debt ratio intact.

LIFE AFTER
A LAYOFF

No job lasts forever, but some of them end before we're ready. (Thank goodness you have that emergency fund ready . . .)

Still, being laid off from a job is hardly something any of us would look forward to. Not only do you have to struggle with the emotional grief and embarrassment that accompanies losing a job, but there's also the sudden drop in income *and* the need to find courage to search for new employment. No wonder the newly jobless often say they experience shock, denial, anger, and frustration in the weeks and months after a pink slip arrives.

So if you find yourself suddenly unemployed, what can you do to turn this bad situation around? Quite a lot, as it turns out.

DON'T LEAVE EMPTY-HANDED

After clearing out your desk, make sure you've had a chance to tie up any loose ends with your former employer. Remember that employment standards legislation sets basic rights in each province, including the right to be adequately notified of a layoff, or to receive severance pay. For terminations without cause (for economic reasons, as opposed to poor performance on the job), termination pay depends on how long you've worked for the company, and lasts up to a maximum of eight weeks.

Your company must also continue your benefits, or compensate for them, during that period. And don't forget that your paycheque must include any vacation pay, sick pay, or overtime owing. Some employers even offer retraining programs and employment counselling. If they're offering it, think about signing up.

Finally, if you think the employer is holding something back, consult employment lawyers. They can tell you if there's anything deficient about the offer.

GET FAMILY FUNDS IN ORDER

Now that you have squared everything away with the former employer, it's time to realistically assess your financial situation at home and create a plan that first outlines any money coming in and money you will be paying out. Start by separating a page into three columns. The first column, "income," might include:

- Employment insurance payments
- Severance pay
- Emergency fund payouts
- Income of a spouse or child
- Interest from savings accounts
- Union aid
- Investment dividends
- Income tax refunds
- Any money coming from a home-based or part-time job

The second column, "expenses," could include:

- Mortgage or rent
- Car payments
- Utilities including heat and hydro
- Cable, telephone, and Internet
- RRSP and other retirement investment payments
- RESP payments
- Insurance payments
- Credit card payments

Now that you know where your money is going, it's time to find ways to cut back expenses until your next job's first paycheque arrives. For instance if you have a mortgage, you may be able to renegotiate your payments so you'll pay less each month until your steady income begins again. (Or take advantage of those "don't pay for one month each year" deals some financial institutions offer.) The upside is that you'll have more money to work with now. The downside is that by paying less today, you'll end up extending the overall lifespan of your mortgage. Still, if you're really struggling, a few extra payments 15 years from now would probably make the move worth it.

A few other ways to reorganize finances include:

- Discontinuing direct payment of bills from your chequing account. Yes, this service was convenient when you had ample money coming in, but right now you need extra flexibility when deciding which bills to pay and when.

- Stopping automatic payments into RRSP investment accounts, RESP education accounts, and any other long-term investments. You need all the money you've got now.

- You may be able to swing a deal with certain utility companies to pay less until you find a job.

- Some cash-value life insurance policies allow the insured to borrow money from them. Ask your agent if this is a possibility for you.

- Figure out which monthly expenses you can actually do without. Swapping your weekly $80 dinner and drink night for a $20 picnic at the park saves $720 during that time. You don't have to live like a miserly hermit, but small changes can equal big savings.

Looking for a silver lining during these tough times? Remember that when you're unemployed, some expenses drop automatically, from your daily lunch and coffee breaks to the need for so many new, stylish skirts to wear five days a week.

BE READY

Is there anything you can do to ensure you're better prepared if it ever happens again? Absolutely. Keep a professional contact list at home (you might not have time to grab it when security is walking you out the door), keep your resumé updated and your network active. And don't forget to network if you think there may be a pink slip in your future. By having plenty of contacts in your industry, you'll stand a better chance of finding work quickly if you lose your job.

NOW BREATHE

Getting a pink slip is an extremely emotional experience and, even in a tough economy, it can come as a shock. While this isn't the time to scream at your boss, sob on her shoulder, or kick cubicle walls, it's okay to recognize what you're feeling— denial, anger, and even sadness—as long as you remain calm and remember that losing your job isn't the end of the world. In fact, many people say that in hindsight, losing a particular job was the best thing that ever happened to them. Really!

LEAVING A LEGACY: DO SOME GOOD

Spend some. Save some. Give some to charity.

Isn't that what we tell our kids when we hand them their allowance for the first time? It's good advice, no matter how old you are. Because chances are you've had the spending thing all wrapped up for ages, and now that you've been boning up on saving strategies and putting them into action, automatic payments come, well, automatically. Now it's time to consider doing some good with a portion of your earnings.

Why? Giving some of your money away to help causes that you believe in transforms communities, whether on your block, or half a world away. Let's face it, not all of us have time to launch a non-profit or hop a plane to volunteer overseas. But even the busiest of us can donate our dollars to a good cause. Charitable giving both changes lives and makes you feel great about being a part of a solution. You'll also feel good about another benefit: the tax write-off.

TAX AID

So long as you get an official tax receipt, you can earn tax credits for most contributions you make to charities. What qualifies? Registered Canadian charities, registered Canadian amateur athletic associations, the United Nations and its related charities, and a few other donees.

Here's how your tax credit is calculated: The first $200 you donate is eligible for a federal tax credit of 15 percent of the donation amount. If you donate more than that, the federal tax credit increases to 29 percent of the amount over the first $200. And don't forget provincial tax credits. In some provinces, they tack on significant credits too.

Donations must be made by December 31 to be claimed against your income in the current year, but you are allowed to pool charitable contributions. If you routinely make donations that equal under $200 per year, hold on to your receipts and make your claim every few years instead to earn the 29 percent.

One more thing to know: if you file your tax return electronically, you must keep your official donation receipts from registered charities or qualified donees in case the Canada Revenue Agency wants to see them. If you file a paper return, however, submit your receipts along with your tax forms. It's also a good idea to hold on to other supporting documents such as cancelled cheques, pledge forms, and credit card statements, in case you're audited.

PROTECT YOURSELF FROM FRAUD

You've probably gotten them—phone calls from people who say they represent charities you've never heard of. Or maybe they're standing at your door asking for a donation. How do you know if the person or charity is legit? Here are a few questions you'll want to ask in order to sort out the real charities from the shams:

1. What is your charity's full name? You should always know exactly who you are donating to, since some fraudsters choose names that are similar to well-known and respected entities.

2. Can you give me written material so I can research you? If the person at the door has no brochure to give you, or at least a card with a website to visit, be wary. Legitimate charitable organizations want to keep donors up to date on what they're doing with their money and the good work being performed, so they always have written material to share. You should never be pressured to donate on the spot. If you are, hang up or close the door. Legit charities don't coerce.

3. Identification please? If you're solicited, ask for the charity's name, address, and telephone number. Then call them and ask if they have a funding drive going on in your area.

4. What is your charity's mission or goal? You can find this information in its annual report, as well as any other pertinent information you'll need to decide if the organization is worthy of receiving your money.

5. Are you a registered charity and will I receive a receipt for tax purposes? It's important to get an official donation receipt in order to claim a tax credit or deduction. Each registered charity has its own specific registration number that must be on your

tax receipt. If you want to confirm that the charity is registered, search for them by name or registration number at the CRA Charities Listings database online or call 1-800-267-2384. You can also call your local branch of the Better Business Bureau to find out if the charity has had any complaints filed against it.

For the latest on the tax implications of charitable giving, visit the Canadian Revenue Agency's website at Cra-arc.gc.ca /charities.

WHERE THERE'S A WILL

Imagine this: you and your husband are packing your bags to take your first vacation to Paris—*sans enfants*—when it suddenly hits you. You don't have a will.

The mind starts churning. What if the plane goes down over the Atlantic? What if one of you chokes on a baguette and dies? What if the worst occurs and you haven't left any written instruction explaining what should happen to your assets and, most importantly, your children, when you're gone? Because, in the end, a will is not so much about the money, but what it will do for the people you leave behind.

So, put up your hand if you have a will. Now, put up your hand if it's up to date. If you don't think you need one because you're single and without dependants, you're wrong. Anyone with assets should have a will. Without one, the province you live in when you die appoints an attorney to use a standard provincial formula to distribute your money and possessions—and determines who gets what. It divides the estate between your spouse, children, and relatives. That means if you had forgotten to revamp your will before finalizing your divorce, it's possible that good-for-nothing soon-to-be-ex could stand to inherit your house, car, or grandma's filigree engagement ring.

Getting the province involved may also result in tying up your money and property for longer as it works its way through the system, leaving your dependants without a way to pay for bills and other expenses in the short term. What's more, provincial rules are not always what you might expect. For example, provincial rules in Alberta dictate that if you have children, they automatically get a slice of the pie too. Your spouse doesn't actually get it all.

Things become even hairier for common-law partners. If you died without a will, your partner might have to provide proof that you were a committed item.

WRITE IT IN

Now that you know why you need one, here's what you'll want to include:

1. The possessions and assets you want distributed

2. Who gets what (your beneficiaries)

3. Who will be your children's guardian, if the kids are minors

4. Who will be your executor (the person or organization you want to administer the estate and carry out your wishes)

Next, write it all down. In most provinces, you'll need it signed by two witnesses in order for the document to become legal. Although there are plenty of do-it-yourself kits available, you'll probably want to hire a lawyer to write the will for you. A bad DIY will may be contested in court, which could turn out to be much more costly in the long run. A simple will, however, can cost as little as $300 in lawyer's fees. If you want to save money, another route is to buy a will kit and use it to answer some of your questions before going to a lawyer, thus streamlining the process.

BUT WHO WILL WATCH THE KIDS?

The question of guardianship is the hardest and most gut-wrenching one for parents with young children. You never think that someone else will be as good a parent as you are, but you'll have to decide who you want to step up to the plate when you're not around. Just remember: you can change your will whenever you want, so if your bachelor brother settles down and marries someone you've grown to love, you can decide to make them guardians rather than hoisting that responsibility onto your ageing mother. Just remember to clear it with everyone first.

Here's one more thing to consider: you can choose more than one person to be a guiding force in your children's lives. For example, you can choose your easygoing brother and sister-in-law to be the kids' guardians, while practical Uncle Andy could be trustee of the estate. By striking this balance, if your daughter suddenly wanted to drop out of school and needed money to backpack around Europe, she'd have to get it from the cash-conscious uncle (and you're sure he'll say no).

Remember that if you've remarried, you'll want to ensure your own kids will inherit part of the estate rather than giving all of your money and property to your new husband. It's easy to see why. That new spouse is under no obligation to give anything to your kids.

Even adult children need to be included in a will, and your decisions must be fair and square or else you'll risk causing fights and alienating siblings. If you do decide to give more money or property to one child, state why. It's hard to argue with someone's last wishes if they seem well thought out—even if you don't agree.

DIVVY IT UP

Get estate-planning advice when it comes time to divide your assets fairly. You might think you're doing your son a favour by leaving him with $100,000 in cash or liquid assets, while your daughter gets your $100,000 RRSP, but you're actually tipping the balance of fairness against him if the estate must pay more taxes before distribution. To keep it even, you'll want to split the investments and give both of your children some of each.

And don't forget bequests. The tradition of handing over money upon our deaths to organizations we believe in goes back centuries. This kind of donation is a good idea for people who want to give more to charities or non-profits during their lives, but feel they don't have the money to give. Take some time to figure out what charities or churches you want to bequest money to and explain why you've made that decision.

No, a will is not something anyone enjoys thinking about, but writing it up and keeping it current sure beats allowing strangers to divide up your estate and decide who gets your kids. So whether you leave all your worldly possessions to your husband, kids, favourite niece, or the Association of Cat Lovers Canada, your will is the best way to safeguard those you love.

BANK ON IT!

Life has a funny way of doing the odd one-eighty. So how often should you review your will with your attorney?

1. Pull out the will with your lawyer every couple of years, for the simple reason that provincial laws can and do change from time to time. You want to be sure that your will is affected only positively by the changes. If not, it's time to rewrite the section influenced by them.

2. Review your will every time there are significant changes in your own life: you have a baby, get married, get divorced, or move out of your province. Remember to set up your power of attorney and a living will too. ∎

CUT THE CLUTTER

Bills. Charitable receipts. Credit card statements. Tax forms. Wills. EI forms. With so much paper entering our homes each week, how do we tame the paper tiger before it consumes us? Wading through disorganized piles of documents can have serious financial consequences if an important piece of paper goes missing or the pile hides a bill due last week. But beyond dollars and cents, disorganization also wastes our precious time and leads to stress. Many people who have a difficult time creating order eventually feel like they can't cope at all.

If it's time for a change, designate an area of your home the "Document Zone," buy a filing cabinet or a stack of three-ring binders, and start tossing what you no longer need. Here's the information you need to make the process run smoothly:

What: Short-term records

When: Hold on to household bills, credit card statements, and receipts for minor purchases for at least three years.

How: To make room for new files, clear out what you no longer need. Chuck statements and receipts that are no longer relevant.

What: Long-term records

When: Keep bank statements, pay stubs, current insurance policies, car documents, house records and mortgage information, tax records, and an inventory of your household goods for at least six years. You may be audited someday.

How: Organize these important documents in a filing cabinet or three-ring binder with ample pockets for smaller pieces of paper. Have binders for your different accounts and tax records (organize each one by year). You can use binders to organize warranty info too. Colour-coding helps keep it all straight.

What: Lifelong records

When: Birth certificates, wills, and power of attorney documents must be kept forever or until they are replaced by a revised file.

How: Again, use cabinets and binders. It's also a good idea to have someone you trust absolutely keep a copy of these documents at his or her home. That way, if your residence is ever destroyed by fire, flood, or high winds, you still have the information you need to apply for new documentation. A lawyer is another good option. Don't leave these crucial documents in a safety deposit box though. If you die, it's not easy for your loved ones to have it opened.

Remember that if you like to keep electronic records of your files, archive them from time to time—and keep a backup so if your system crashes, you'll still have your data. It's also a smart idea to set up a binder or file that outlines the location of all of your important files. Let one or two people know exactly where this binder is so they're not looking for it when dealing with an emergency. Include:

- Your legal name
- Your Social Insurance Number
- Your date and place of birth
- Your legal address and names of spouse and children
- The location of your will, insurance policies, bank accounts, and name of your lawyer
- Location of your birth, divorce, and citizenship certificates
- Employment information
- Names and addresses of close friends and doctors
- Requests and preferences for you burial and funeral

YOUR TWO CENTS

You did it. You've read through the chapters of this book, either page by page or by flipping to the sections most relevant to your life. You've learned how to earn the money you deserve, spend money intelligently, and steadily save what you need to live life fabulously today and well into your future. And now you're only a page away from finding out how you can take all the tips, tricks, and smart advice you've picked up, and apply them to your practical, hassle-free, month-by-month money plan to get you on your way.

You're almost there.

Chapter 9

YOUR
SIX-MONTH
MONEY PLAN

....

MORTGAGES. CAR LOANS. RRSPs AND INVESTMENT portfolios. Emergency funds. Life and home insurance. Budgeting and wills. It's all enough to make the head spin.

But here's the good news: the hardest part of building wealth is simply getting started. Once you have a plan, everything else falls into place. As we finally move into this short, but incredibly powerful chapter, we're going to remove the guesswork from deciding which tasks to tackle first through last so you feel comfortable and even excited about managing your money well.

Why a six-month money checklist and not a six-week? Let's be honest about what it takes to forge ahead with planning for the rest of your financial life. It takes time. Not eight-hour days mind you, but at least a few hours each week need to be set aside for dreaming, dealing with banks and investment firms, web research, calculating, and, if you choose, talking to financial planners and accountants.

We know you're supremely busy, but finding just two or three hours a week now will buy you years of worry-free time later.

Even so, remember that the Six-Month Plan is merely a guide. And although we'll give you a list of high-priority goals for each month, only you know what is most important to your family and your life. So if you are already debt-free or you refinanced your mortgage last week, go ahead and tick off those boxes right from the start.

Whatever your story, this plan will help you take action, build momentum, and set realistic financial goals.

MONTH

1

LAY THE FOUNDATION

NAVEL GAZE. First things first. Before you take on smart earning, spending, and saving, please ask yourself some crucially important money questions. There is absolutely no point in embarking on the path to, say, debt reduction without understanding what motivates you to buy in the first place. Here are a few questions to get you started:

- How did my parents deal with money? Was it talked about in our house or not? Did my parents or other respected adults ever explain money matters to me when I was young?

- During my childhood, did my family struggle financially or did I always feel there was enough money to spend? How did this affect me?

- What is my definition of rich? How much money do I think I need in order to feel wealthy? Why?

- How do I make financial decisions? Research and more research? Ask people I respect for opinions? Go with my gut?

- Why am I working in my current job? Am I doing what I always dreamed of or am I living Plan B? If so, what is forcing me to stay?

- How would I feel about asking for a raise or hiking my rates? Why?

- Do I think couples should have joint or separate bank accounts? Why?
- How do I feel when I shop? Anxious that I'm spending money or do I experience a high every time I slap down a credit card?
- Have I ever avoided bills or ATM slips? If so, why?
- How do I picture myself at age 65?

WHAT MOTIVATES YOUR OTHER HALF? If you are in a serious relationship or are married, ask your partner to answer the same questions then compare results. You'll learn why both of you handle money the way you do, and you can use the information to blaze a financial trail together in the coming months.

CUT THE CLUTTER. Are your papers a mess? Take a few hours this month—break it up into easy 30-minute chunks if you must—and sort, file, and throw away. See Chapter 8 for ideas about what to keep and for how long. Have you found a stash of unpaid and overdue bills or credit card statements? Make paying at least the minimum balance a top priority this month.

TAKE THE SIX-MONTH CHANGE CHALLENGE. Saving money doesn't have to be drudgery, and what better way to watch it grow than storing your investment in a clear jar? Throw a toonie in the jar each day (your family can drop them in too) to make it a habit.

MONTH

2

TRACK IT DOWN

TRACK SPENDING. Try to keep track of your spending habits over a couple of weeks to a month to discover where exactly your money is going. Flip back to page 46 to find out how it's done. Track your spending and it will help you with the next stage: budgeting.

KNOW WHAT YOU OWE. If you've been letting the numbers creep up on credit cards, lines of credit, and within consolidated loans, be ready for a nasty shock. But don't despair! By understanding how much debt you have, you're making a first step toward driving it back down. Revisit page 92 and use our "How much do I owe?" worksheet to get a lay of the land.

KNOW WHAT YOU HAVE: What is your household income? How about home equity, RRSPs, and other investments? Subtract what you owe from what you have to determine your net worth and how far into the black or red you really are.

GET YOUR CREDIT SCORE. Unsure what your credit score is? It's time to fire up your computer and check the credit bureaus' websites or reach for the phone and find out. With a great score, you'll be offered—and be able to negotiate—better deals from mortgages to credit card rates. Contact the two main credit-reporting agencies: TransUnion and Equifax at Transunion.ca and Equifax.ca.

HIRE A PLANNER. If you decide to sign up for some professional financial help, start by asking money-savvy friends which planner they use, or try checking Fpsccanada.org, the Financial Planners Standards Council's database of planners across Canada. Only those in good standing are listed.

JOIN A MONEY CLUB. You don't have to be a financial wiz to participate in a money club. Simply grab a few people who want to get their finances on track and meet up once a month. Visit Chatelaine.com for tips and advice.

STATE OF THE UNION. At least once a month (or even more often in the first few months) sit down and go over the books either by yourself or with your spouse. Make it a quasi-date night if that makes the prospect seem more exciting. And don't forget to keep throwing your toonies in the jar.

MONTH

3

MAKE A CHANGE

SET A BUDGET BATTLE PLAN. Evaluate the spending patterns you tracked last month and come up with goals for saving. Keep tracking and stay within your guidelines. Can't remember how? Turn back to page 44 for a budget refresher course.

ESTABLISH A SYSTEM FOR PAYING BILLS. Do your bills often go unopened or do you simply forget to pay on time? Designate one area of your home "Bill Central" and set up a plan so you're paying them off each month. Find out more on page 54.

TAME YOUR DEBT. Searching for a way to incur less credit card interest? While the most effective way is to pay off your purchases in full each month, that's not always an option if you're digging yourself out of debt today. Turn back to Chapter 3 to pick up smart solutions for driving down debt.

GET TAXES IN ORDER. No one likes to think about taxes, but if you're behind in filing them, or RRSP season is upon you, gather up the files and set aside a couple of hours per week this month until the deed is done. Read Chapter 5 to pick up some good advice.

MONTH

4

SAVE
FOR LIFE

UNCOVER YOUR EARNINGS. Take a good look at your career and ask yourself if you are where you want to be right now. Are you making enough money to pay your bills and keep a roof over your head (about 50 percent of what you bring in)? Are you saving a chunk in an emergency fund for retirement and other long- and short-term goals (about 20 percent)? And are you having some fun (think 30 percent for entertainment, vacations, dinners out, gifts, etc.)? If not, maybe you can find ways to make more without totally exhausting yourself. Check to see what kind of benefits you get. Are they adequate? If not, perhaps you can you ask for better or more relevant ones. Devise a plan and approach your manager if the timing seems right. Head back to Chapter 1 for more work-related suggestions.

SET UP RRSPs, RESPs, AND YOUR INVESTMENT PORT-FOLIO. We're not saying you have to start loading up on stocks, bonds, and other investment vehicles. This month you should simply be laying the foundation for a smart and sensible plan. Sign up for automatic payments and begin at your own pace. Even $200 a month earning five percent interest will add up to $31,056 in 10 short years. This month, it's all about making saving a habit. Check out Chapter 4 for some hassle-free, low-stress investment ideas. If you feel the time is right to become more aggressive, that's perfectly fine too. Take this month to research your options.

Remember to stick to the toonie-a-day goal.

MONTH

5

PLAN FOR EMERGENCIES

START AN EMERGENCY FUND OR FUNDS. Most experts agree that you should have between three and six months' worth of living expenses put aside to help you prepare for life's emergencies such as job loss, fire, and serious illness. Approach your financial institution and open a savings account. Then get in the habit of making regular deposits weekly, biweekly, or monthly. Once you feel you can start adding more, up your contributions. See page 243 for more ideas.

GET INSURED. Buy home insurance, life insurance, car insurance, and others. Do you have enough? Do your research then approach an insurance agent referred by friends or colleagues. Some financial advisors can handle these transactions as well.

WRITE A WILL. Get over the squeamish factor and just do it. See page 252 to find out how.

MONTH

6

ALMOST DONE

MAKE YOUR HOME WORK FOR YOU. Do you pour good money into your house only to watch it eat up all your extra cash? If your mortgage term is almost up, think about refinancing your house to lower the interest and save hundreds or thousands of dollars. Take advantage of government tax credit programs too, and make some necessary repairs to lower your heating costs, make the place more comfortable, or ready your home to be put on the market.

CHECK IN ON DEBT. You've been snowballing your debt payments for months now. Do you have any credit cards paid off in full yet? It might be time to call the credit card company and either lower your rate or cancel the card outright (as long as it's a newer card, so closing it will have less of an impact on your credit score).

KEEP UP TO DATE. Between interest rate roller coasters and ever-adjusting tax legislation, finance info changes on a dime. Keep tabs on new rules, regulations, and information by bookmarking some of your favourite money sites.

TALK ABOUT MONEY. Now that your debt is down, savings are up, bills are being paid on time, and taxes are filed, sit down with a journal or around the kitchen table with family members and explore how the last six months have changed you—and where you're headed. Break out the bubbly and spend those toonies. If you have kids, let them roll the coins and exchange them at the bank for bills. It's time to put the money saved toward pure, unadulterated fun.

You've earned it.

LEARN MORE

••

Do you want to find out more about earning, spending, or saving? Consult the following online resources to glean extra information about specific aspects of money management.

CALCULATE IT!

CANADA SALARY CALCULATOR
Canadavisa.com/canada-salary-wizard.html

CHATELAINE'S FINANCIAL CALCULATORS & TOOLS
Chatelaine.com

TAX-FREE SAVINGS ACCOUNT NUMBER CRUNCHER
Budget.gc.ca/2008/mm/calc_e.html

EARN IT!

CANADA BENEFITS
Canadabenefits.gc.ca

CANADIAN LABOUR CONGRESS
Canadianlabour.ca

HUMAN RESOURCES AND SKILLS DEVELOPMENT CANADA
Hrsdc.gc.ca

INNOVISIONS CANADA AND CANADIAN TELEWORK ASSOCIATION
Ivc.ca

JOB BANK
Jobbank.gc.ca

JOB FUTURES
Jobfutures.ca

JOBS IN CANADA
Jobsincanada.com

MONSTER
Monster.ca

SECOND CAREER ONTARIO
Secondcareerontario.com

WOMEN IN CANADA: WORK CHAPTER UPDATES (STATISTICS CANADA)
Statcan.gc.ca/pub/89f0133x/89f0133x2006000-eng.htm

WORK-LIFE BALANCE
Hrsdc.gc.ca/eng/lp/spila/wlb/01home.shtml

WORKOPOLIS
Workopolis.com

SPEND IT!

CANADA REVENUE AGENCY
Cra-arc.gc.ca

CANADA MORTGAGE AND HOUSING CORPORATION
Cmhc-schl.gc.ca

CANADIAN AUTOMOBILE ASSOCIATION
Caa.ca

CANADIAN CONSUMER INFORMATION GATEWAY
Consumerinformation.ca

EQUIFAX
Equifax.ca

FRUGAL SHOPPER CANADA
Frugalshopper.ca

INSURANCE BUREAU OF CANADA
Ibc.ca

REVENU QUÉBEC
Revenu.gouv.qc.ca

SAVE.CA
Save.ca

TRANSUNION
Transunion.ca

UNIVERSAL CHILD CARE BENEFIT
Cra-arc.gc.ca/benefits

SAVE IT!

ADVOCIS
Advocis.ca

ALBERTA SECURITIES COMMISSION
Albertasecurities.com

AUTORITÉ DES MARCHÉS FINANCIERS
Lautorite.qc.ca

BANK OF CANADA
Bank-banque-canada.ca

BRITISH COLUMBIA SECURITIES COMMISSION
Bcsc.bc.ca

CANADIAN BANKERS ASSOCIATION
Yourmoney.cba.ca

CANADIAN BUSINESS ONLINE
Canadianbusiness.com

CANLEARN
Canlearn.ca

CPP INVESTMENT BOARD
Cppib.ca

FINANCIAL PLANNERS STANDARDS COUNCIL
Fpsccanada.org

INDUSTRY CANADA
Ic.gc.ca

INVESTMENT INDUSTRY REGULATORY ORGANIZATION OF CANADA
Iiroc.ca

INVESTOR EDUCATION FUND
Investored.ca

MANITOBA SECURITIES COMMISSION
Msc.gov.mb.ca

MONTREAL EXCHANGE
M-x.ca

MORNINGSTAR
Morningstar.ca

NEW BRUNSWICK SECURITIES COMMISSION
Nbsc-cvmnb.ca

NOVA SCOTIA SECURITIES COMMISSION
Gov.ns.ca/nssc/

ONTARIO SECURITIES COMMISSION
Osc.gov.on.ca

PEI SECURITIES OFFICE
Gov.pe.ca/securities

SASKATCHEWAN FINANCIAL SERVICES COMMISSION
Sfsc.gov.sk.ca

SECURITIES COMMISSION OF NEWFOUNDLAND AND LABRADOR
Gs.gov.nl.ca/cca/fsr/

SMALL INVESTOR PROTECTION ASSOCIATION
Sipa.ca

THE INVESTMENT FUNDS INSTITUTE OF CANADA
Ific.ca

TORONTO STOCK EXCHANGE & TSX VENTURE EXCHANGE
Tmx.com

INDEX

A

adoption, parental benefits, 225, 227
air conditioners, 63–65
Alberta
    estate planning, 252
    maternity leave, 224
amateur athletic associations, 249
amortization, 176
appliances, 61
Ashlie, Taylore, 80
assets in estate planning, 251–254
auditors, 161–162
automobiles. *see* cars

B

bad debt, 80–83
bank accounts
    for couples, 209–211
    cutting costs, 60–61
    fees, 65, 90
Bank of Canada, 79
bankruptcy, 101–104
benefits
    employer top-ups, 226–227

negotiating, 17, 37–38
    parental, 224–229
bequests, 254
bills
    payment strategies, 54–59
    retention of records, 255
British Columbia, divorce settlements, 205
budgets
    after layoff, 246–247
    developing, 44–54
    six-month money plan, 259–273
burnout, 23–28
businesses. *see* self-employment
buying
    cars, 69–72
    developing a budget, 44–54
    exchange or refund, 68–69
    money saving strategies, 68–69
    see also homes, purchasing

C

Canada Child Tax Benefit, 147
Canada Education Savings Grant (CESG),
    232–233, 235

Canada Mortgage and Housing
Corporation (CMHC), 173
Canada Pension Plan, death benefits, 237
Canada Post, 57
Canadian Consumer Alert (Foran), 62
Canadian Telework Association, 20
CareerBuilder.com, 36
careers
  advancing, 29–37
  balance in, 7–11, 14, 268
  flextime, 18–22
  higher-earning spouses, 211
  layoff, 245–248
  negotiating pay and benefits, 37–38
  negotiating raises, 10, 15–16
  sabbaticals, 23–29
  see also self-employment
Caregiver Tax Credit, 147–148
Carpenter, Kira and Doug, 230
Carroll-Foster, Katrina, 44
cars
  insurance, 241, 242
  maintenance, 66–67
  purchase or lease, 69–72
cash advance loans, 100
cash advances, 86
Centre for Families, Work and Well-Being,
  20
Certified General Accountants Association
  of Canada, 79
charitable donations, 151, 248–251, 254
cheque advance loans, 100
cheques, convenience, 86
children
  in divorces, 213, 218
  education, 231–236
  expenses, 230–231
  guardianship of, 252–253
  maternity leave, 223–229
  taxes deductions and, 146–147
Children's Fitness Tax Credit, 147
common-law marriages, 217–218, 252
  see also spouses
commuting expenses, 150
convenience cheques, 86
cooking, money saving strategies for,
  61–63
cooling costs, 63–65
couch potato investors, 132–133
couples
  differing financial styles, 197–203, 262
  joint finances, 209–211
coupons, 63, 68
credit cards
  bill payment, 55
  choosing, 84

debt and, 79–84
fees, 65, 85–89, 93
interest rates, 82–83
retention of records, 255
credit limits, 87
credit rating, 97–99, 101, 169
credit unions, 60
critical illness insurance, 237–238, 239–240

D

daycare, 146
death benefits, 237
debit cards, 90
debt
  credit and, 79–84
  good vs. bad, 80–83
  strategies to decrease, 91–97, 124
deferral deposit loans, 100
depression, divorce and, 217
disability insurance, 241
diversity in the workplace, 12–13
divorce
  in common-law marriages, 218
  pre-nuptial agreements and, 204–207
  preparing for, 212–217
  settlements, 205
divorce mediators, 213–214
documents, 255–256
dollar-cost averaging, 126

E

earning a living. *see* work
ecoENERGY Retrofit program, 149
education, 231–236
emergency funds, 243–244, 270
employers
  disability insurance, 241
  maternity top-up benefits, 226–227
employment. *see* work
Employment Insurance (EI), 224, 226–227,
  229
energy costs, 63–65
Equifax, 98
Ernst & Young, 12
estate planning, 251–254
exchange of purchases, 73–75
exchange-traded funds (ETFs), 132
expenditures, tracking, 44–54

F

Facebook, 31, 36
Families and Work Institute, 20
family, balancing work and, 7–11, 14
Family Life and Work Life (Sauvé), 8
fees
  banks, 60, 65, 158

car lease, 70
credit cards, 65, 84–89
credit rating and, 97
debit cards, 90
financial planners, 108–109, 111–112
home purchase, 114, 180
investments, 95, 132, 133
late fees, 57–59
payday loans, 100
tax professionals, 141
tuition, 147, 232
FICO (Fair Isaac Corporation) score, 97–99
financial planners
    benefits of, 106–109
    choosing, 110–113
    for couples, 201–202
financial plans, six-month, 259–273
fitness, taxes deductions and, 147
flextime, 18–22
food, money saving strategies for, 61–63
Foran, Pat, 62
fraud, 250–251
funeral costs, 237

G
good debt, 80–83
Google, 36
groceries, money saving strategies for, 61–63
gross debt service (GDS) ratio, 170
Groundbreakers report, 12
group RESP plans, 234
guardianship, 252–253

H
H & R Block, 141
health care, 67–68
health insurance, 237–239
heating costs, 63–65
Hedge Fund Research, 125
Hewitt Associates, 24
Home Buyers' Plan, 135, 172–173
Home Buyers' Tax Credit, 149–150
Home Renovation Tax Credit, 148–149
homes
    children and, 230
    insurance, 240
    records of possessions, 255
    renovations, 148–149
homes, purchasing
    closing costs, 180–181
    decision to purchase, 165–171
    down payment, 171–172
    first-time buyers, 149–150
    inspectors, 179–180
    real estate agents, 177–178, 184–185
    terminology, 189–195

see also mortgages
homes, selling, 184–188
hospitals, 67–68
house insurance, 240
husbands. *see* spouses
Hyman, Lisa, 2

I
inactivity fees, 87–88
index funds, 132
ING DIRECT, 60, 243
insurance
    choosing, 236–238
    evaluating, 66, 242, 271
    importance of, 235–236
    retention of records, 255
    types of, 238–241
Insurance Bureau of Canada, 240, 241
interest rates
    bill payment and, 57
    credit cards, 55, 65, 82–85, 93
    on mortgages, 174–176
    online banks, 60
interviews, 33–35
investments
    goals, 123–124, 269
    money clubs, 121–123
    options, 131–137
    risk, 125–126
    strategies, 126–131
    terminology, 115–120
    see also financial planners

J
joint accounts, 209–210

K
Kirkland, Christine, 18
KPMG, 227

L
layoffs, 245–248
leasing cars, 69–72
leaves, maternity, 223–229
leaves of absence, 23–29
Lehman Brothers, 113
life insurance, 237, 239–240, 247
lines of credit, 94
LinkedIn, 31
loans
    consolidated, 93
    from family, 94
    payday, 100
    for RRSPs, 95
    see also mortgages
Loose Change Inc., 46

M

Macpherson, Ross, 33, 34
Maritz Research, 187
marriage
　joint finances, 209–211
　pre-nuptial agreements, 204–207
　wedding expenses, 207–209
　see also spouses
marriage contracts, 204
maternity benefits, 224–229
maternity leave, 223–229
McMillan, Kathy, 109–110
mediation, divorce, 213–214
medical expenses, 150–151
Mills, Amanda, 46, 47, 200
money clubs, 121–123
money plans, six-month, 259–273
moonlighting, 22
mortgages
　amortization period, 176
　amount of, 182
　biweekly payments, 66
　credit history and, 169
　down payment, 171–172
　as good debt, 80–82
　paying down quickly, 181–184
　pre-approval, 173–174
　refinancing, 94
　renegotiating payments, 247
　retention of records, 255
　terminology, 189–195
　types of, 174–176
motivation, 261–262
moving expenses, 150
mutual funds, 126–127, 132–133

N

National Center for Women and
　Retirement Research, 106
National Population Health Survey,
　212
Natural Resources Canada, 64
networking, 30–32, 248
New Brunswick, small claims court, 75
non-scholarship RESP plans, 234
Nuance Occasions, 207

O

online bill payments, 57
online self-marketing, 37
Ontario
　divorce settlements, 205
　refund of purchases, 73
　small claims court, 75
Overcoming Underearning (Stanny), 11

P

Pagnutti, Lou, 12
parental benefits, 224–229
parental leave, 223–229
parents, caring for, 147–148
partners. *see* spouses
pay
　higher-earning spouses, 211
　negotiating a raise, 10, 15–16
　negotiating in a new job, 37–38
payday loans, 100
personal life, balance in, 7–11, 14
personal money style, 201
Pinsky, Erica, 10
pooled RESP plans, 234
post-dated cheque loans, 100
post-marital agreements, 204
power of attorney, 254, 256
pre-authorized payments, 58
pre-nuptial agreements, 204–207
President's Choice Financial, 65
prospectuses, 126–127
purchases
　cars, 69–72
　developing a budget, 44–54
　exchange or refund, 73–75
　money saving strategies, 68–69
　see also homes, purchasing

Q

Quebec
　adoptive parent benefits, 227
　common-law marriages, 217
　parental benefits, 224–225
Quebec Parental Insurance Plan (QPIP),
　224, 225, 226–227

R

real estate agents, 177–178, 184–185
receipts, 145
records, 255–256
refund of purchases, 73–75
renting, 170–171
RESPs (Registered Education Savings
　Plans), 231–236
resumés, 33, 34, 37, 248
retirement, planning, 128–131
Richardson Partners Financial Limited, 109
Royal Canadian Mounted Police, 226
Royal LePage Canada, 170, 187
RRSPs (Registered Retirement Savings Plans)
　borrowing for home purchase, 171–172
　as investment, 134–135
　to pay off debt, 94–95
　taxes and, 146, 153–156